THE HAPPINESS BOOK

THE HAPPINESS BOOK

Danny Danziger

with photographs by

Nic Barlow

PAN ORIGINAL

Pan Books London and Sydney

A percentage of the author's royalties from the sale of this book will be donated to the Royal College of Nursing.

First published 1980 by Pan Books Ltd,
Cavaye Place, London SW10 9PG

ISBN 0 330 26208 4
Printed in Great Britain by R. J. Acford
Industrial Estate
Chichester, Sussex

THE HAPPINESS BOOK

There is no duty we so much underrate as the duty of being happy.
ROBERT LOUIS STEVENSON

Happiness: a good bank account, a good cook, and a good digestion.
JEAN-JACQUES ROUSSEAU

A lifetime of happiness! No man alive could bear it: it would be hell on earth.
BERNARD SHAW, *Man and Superman*

A man is never as unhappy as he thinks, nor as happy as he had hoped.
LA ROCHEFOUCAULD, *Maximes Supprimées*

All who joy would win
Must share it – happiness was born a twin.
BYRON, *Don Juan*

O happiness! our being's end and aim!
Good, Pleasure, Ease, Content! whate'er thy name,
That something still: which prompts th'eternal sigh,
For which we bear to live, or dare to die.
POPE, *Essay on Man*

Contents

Derek Jameson
Koko
Angela Lambert
Dennis Lane
Commander Roger Lane-Nott
John Levis
Stan Lomax
Lord Longford
Joe Loss
Michael McCrum
Charles McFadyen
Sue MacGregor
Norris McWhirter
Eric Malpass
Yehudi Menuhin
Keith Miller
Patrick Moore
Sir Jeremy Morse
Jack Morton
Lance-Corporal Joss Murray
Alice Anne Parker
Sister Georgina Payne

Jim Pearce
Len Penrose
Mary Peters
Sheila Pickles
Enoch Powell
Marje Proops
Magnus Pyke
Mary Rathmell
Frances Robinson
Harry Secombe
David Shilling
Alistair Sinclair
David Steel
Erin Stratton
Sheila Walker
The Duke of Westminster
Barbara Wieshoff
James Alfred Wight
Frederick Trevor Woods
Mike Worden
Bill Wright
Father Xmas

Introduction

On a cold, leaden-grey and rainy afternoon, with the wind howling mournfully around my windowpanes while the candles flickered sullenly in my room during the winter's second electricity blackout, I contemplated the nature of happiness. The daily papers were less than encouraging on the subject, with hints of industrial strife, suggestions of future wars and promises of greater catastrophes to come. With world developments progressing the way they do, it seemed improbable that we could expect a radical change of policy on any front. 'Today the Inland Revenue has decided to abolish income tax and reimburse taxpayers for their past fifty years of payment.' Or, 'The Meteorological Office announces that over the next twelve months the weather will be a mild and sunny 18°C. It will only rain for farmers.' Unlikely.

There are times when happiness seems as alien a commodity as red dust from Mars. Surely we want, expect, hope for a little happiness in our 72.4 years on this planet. If someone could isolate the secret of happiness, patent it and give it to the world, imagine how things would take a turn for the better.

I once asked five people what happiness meant to them. I got five different answers, ranging from contentment or the absence of pain to joy and ecstasy. That was a clue. Happiness is a feeling that is experienced at different emotional levels. It can be brought on by something relatively simple and mundane like a beautiful sunrise or a loved one's smile, or not until one has solved the more complex problems of life itself.

So would it follow that what makes the more intelligent or educated person happy is more sophisticated or unobtainable than that which makes someone with less intelligence happy? Within time I found out. A manual worker on a factory line has the same hopes for his cerebrally retarded daughter as the film producer has for his cerebrally retarded son. And yet, with the uniqueness of each individual, the upbringing, family and experiences that mould the human character, it is unlikely that two people will have the same dreams, aspirations and idea of happiness.

The striving for happiness is one of the most fundamental human urges. The American Declaration of Independence considers the pursuit of happiness as important as life itself, and thunders in the very first sentence: 'We hold these truths to be self-evident; that all men are created equal; that they are endowed by their Creator with certain unalienable rights; that among these are life, liberty, and the pursuit of happiness.'

As the idea for this book crystallized in my mind, I knew that photographs would make it come alive. I couldn't even load film into a camera, but Nic could – I'd seen his work and thought it was great. Nic and I got on exceptionally well, and our friendship made the whole project seem even less like work.

When we first started interviewing people, I would simply ask outright, 'What makes you happy?' turn on my tape recorder and wait for the words to flow. Sometimes they didn't. It was just too inhibiting – a perfect stranger asking an intimate question and expecting an immediate answer. So at times I would take down their response in shorthand, or ask them to write down what makes them happy.

Not everyone agreed to be interviewed, however. Once we said we were writing a book on happiness, reactions differed enormously. Some would act as if we were the vanguard of a preposterous new religion and hurry away. Others would wink suggestively and nudge the air with a salacious thrust. On one occasion in Glasgow, we were steered towards a chimney-sweep called Ernie, a man without whose contribution we were assured our book would be incomplete. Ernie was seated behind a desk. I asked him the usual question and almost immediately, with a roar of anger, his face twisted and flushed with hate; this less than jolly giant, all 6 feet 5 inches of him, sprang up from his chair with a look so promising of homicidal intentions that Nic and I ran for our lives, leaving a camera and tape recorder in his office. We never found out what makes Ernie happy.

That incident was the exception. We were invariably greeted at people's homes and working-places with every friendship and kindness. We must have drunk a thousand cups of tea. The army were excellent hosts in Belfast, giving us our own escort, and the navy put a nuclear submarine in Plymouth at our disposal.

There were times when it was uplifting to meet people with whom you wouldn't normally associate happiness: Mike Worden, an undertaker, and a thoroughly amiable man; David Bickers, one of the most severely disabled of the thalidomides, and with an enviable zest for life and a determination to succeed.

It was often difficult or complicated to arrange an interview or photograph. We were appalled when the Heathrow Airport authorities said we needed a minimum of one million pounds' public liability insurance in order to step on the tarmac to photograph stewardess Jeanette Hartley in front of Concorde. We were all prepared to abandon the interview until we learned that the premium is only around £5. We sat through five hours of preliminary judging of the heats for Mr Britain (the ultimate body-building title) until Roy Duval got on stage. He won the title, but if I never see a tricep or pectoral muscle again, I shan't mind. We clambered ninety metres down a coal mine to meet Jack Morton, and I had to juggle with four mining hats, safety lights turned on, so that Nic could take his picture in the pitch-black shaft. With ink on his fingers, Chris Bonington was well into his next book and clearly didn't want to see us when we arrived at his remote Cumbrian farmhouse. Still he did talk to us for half an hour. And the only time Laura Ashley could find to talk to me was on her private plane, so I had a most enjoyable weekend trip to France.

Each person we met meant a new and exhilarating experience. Sergeant Woods, a Chelsea Pensioner, stood us a pint of beer in the Royal Hospital mess, and a more friendly or rowdy group of men you will never find. Alistair Henderson took us to the top of his lighthouse in the Outer Hebrides and we talked about life for the best part of a day. Harry Secombe gave us each a rare book; Alan Ayckbourn gave us seats to the opening night of his latest play; and Robin Batchelor took us up in his balloon, where for a blissful afternoon we floated high above Bedfordshire, letting the wind control our direction.

This book gave us an opportunity to meet a great many interesting and remarkable people. Some we will see once more, others may never cross our paths again. We always felt a sharp sadness in saying goodbye – to enter someone's life and ask them to reveal intimacies they may have never even thought about and then to leave somehow seemed ungrateful. Nic and I always thought it had been a privilege to know them.

With the number of people in the book it's impossible to tell anecdotes about them all. But there are a few magical memories that I shall never forget. In the Rhondda valley in mid Glamorgan the Treorchy male voice choir practises in the junior school's gymnasium once a week. We came across them by chance and told them about our happiness book. Ninety Welsh voices exploded into laughter and then they sang for us a Welsh song about happiness. It was the sweetest sound I ever heard. One Friday we asked Mrs Lewin, the headmistress of the Holmwood School in Salisbury, if we could pick out some of her children to find out what makes them happy. She told us to come back on Monday, when we were greeted by the whole school singing for us 'I Can Sing a Rainbow'. A hundred adorable children, aged from 4 to 9, most of them singing in uncharted keys, and yet it sounded to us quite magical. Finally, I shall never forget meeting the Commissioner of the Salvation Army, ninety-seven-year-old Catherine Bramwell-Booth, and her two sisters Olive and Dorothy. Their enthusiasm and goodness left us ashamed of our rude worldliness.

It would appear that happiness is a highly subjective emotion. Each person we spoke to redefined the word on a different, esoteric level, and there seems to be no limit to the articulacy and sincerity of our contributors. In the final analysis, money is apparently an unimportant commodity in the obtainment of happiness. Several people spoke of a moment in their lives when, for no logical reason, they felt an overwhelming happiness, a freeze-frame memory of never repeated intensity. It may have come playing in the garden as a child or just walking down the street, but they remembered it as a moment of which they could say later, I was happy then.

There is one school of thought which believes that happiness can only be understood and enjoyed after great sadness. I hope they're not right. It reminds me of the old joke: 'Why are you banging your head against the wall?' 'Because it feels so good when I stop.'

Undeniably, the single most recurring theme is having someone to love, someone to share happiness with. And the most fundamental disagreement is whether happiness should be, or can be, pursued. But many people think that happiness, if it does exist for them, is no more than a byproduct of life itself.

When you look through this book you will see happiness redefined over and over again. To John Levis, the innkeeper, happiness is halfway between cheerfulness and ecstasy; to Cleeve Arscott, the beekeeper, it is a stage beyond contentment, and to the ropemaker, Peter Annison, happiness is a stage at one end of the emotional spectrum, with gloom, despair and despondency at the other.

No one can define happiness conclusively, that's something I've learned, but through this book I can *show* you what makes people happy, a sort of empirical definition – with people from all walks of life as the reference points.

Danny Danziger
June 1980

Note on Photography

For many of the subjects of this book, it must have been quite an ordeal to have my awesome cameras staring at them, with a large lighting system behind. On the whole everyone coped admirably. Some of the photographs were easy to do as there was ample time to work out the shot, set up the lighting and have dramatic props; others were quite the reverse.

A successful portrait is not just a case of getting the exposure right and producing a good print with dense blacks – it must capture the *soul* of the sitter. While most people were pleased with my pictures of them, there were one or two who were far from thrilled – indeed, one irate letter arrived demanding that the negatives and prints should be destroyed immediately. This made me feel a bit low until an enlightened friend pointed out that a good portrait does not just play up to the vanity of the sitter; other considerations come into it.

I used two camera systems to produce the photographs – Hassleblad (with 50, 80 and 150 mm lenses and the Hassleblad SWC) and Canon (C17, 24, 35, 50, 85, 135 mm). The film used throughout was Ilford FP4 and HP5 which I processed in Perceptol. The prints were made on Ilfospeed Pearl.

Nic Barlow
June 1980

Hardy Amies

The Queen's vivid pink Jubilee outfit and Broadmoor wardens' uniform have one thing in common. They were both designed by Hardy Amies who has filled the gap in between these extremes with uniforms for the Stock Exchange guides, the Oxford boat crew and British Airways. Hardy Amies wasn't always in fashion. Failing to win a scholarship to Cambridge, he moved to France and Germany, becoming fluent in both languages. When he returned to England, he was hired as a travelling salesman for a weighing machine company and won a gold trophy for his skill as a salesman. During the war, as head of Belgian intelligence Hardy Amies was trained to organize sabotage in occupied countries. He has designed clothes for the Queen since 1950 and is now also regarded as the leading designer of menswear in the world. Recently Hardy Amies has turned his designing hand to the home and has produced everything from towels to loo brushes. His biggest venture is a washable wallpaper, not for the Crown this time, but for Crown. So if you don't want to wear Hardy Amies you can paste him up on your walls.

Happiness must mean that the resources of creation and the savouring of sensations of touch, taste and smell, must be used carefully during the few years which compose a human life. Waste is the enemy of happiness. Money brings happiness because it gives you the means to express yourself – in your house, your clothes and in your way of life. Some people can only express themselves by accumulating money for its own sake. Artists are lucky; their ways are clearly signposted.

Happiness is the calm which comes after self-expression has been achieved. This calm gives you the opportunity to help the young and inexperienced and the old and frustrated, to try to fulfil themselves. This is the last and greatest happiness.

Peter Annison

How many knots can you tie? Five? Ten? Peter Annison, a ropemaker in the beautiful Yorkshire Dales market town of Hawes, knows how to tie hundreds. With a degree in textile chemistry, which he used to teach at Nottingham University, Peter is putting his knowledge to practical use.

There are many different types of knots. Butchers, fishermen, sailors, lorry drivers, mountaineers all adapt knots for their particular needs, and although we now use synthetic ropes of nylon more often than natural fibres, rope still remains an essential commodity for many jobs. Peter makes bell ropes for churches, cow ties and halters for the farmers in his community, skipping ropes, hammocks and shopping bags. The list of products he can make from rope is endless.

Rope is one of the earliest materials made by man, who probably got the idea from plaited creepers in the forest. Fishing nets were made of rope more than 5,000 years ago, and the ancient sailors needed rope to raise sails and moor ships. And rope was used in crude pulleys for a mechanical device to raise weights heavier than a man could carry.

Happiness is a state at one end of the emotional spectrum with gloom, despair and despondency at the other, and all the other points needed as a frame of reference. Happiness is being able to stay at the right end of the spectrum for longer than you stay at the other end.

Much has been said and written about the soul-destroying nature of repetitive work and how this contributes to the industrial strife in the country. Now, we have not found this to be true. Much of our work is repetitious and yet it can be strangely soothing to get into a gentle rhythm and see the rope piling up towards the batch size of 50. As my colleague Norman said the other day, 'You even find it difficult to know at which point in the cycle to break off to go to the loo.'

Ultimately happiness at work seems to boil down to doing something useful in the sense that others want the fruits of your efforts and depend upon them. In our case, the measure of this is the full order book and a healthy balance sheet. As Jim Slater said, 'Money is not an end in itself (in business), it is just the score sheet.'

Cleeve Arscott

Cleeve Arscott remembers watching his grandfather, who kept bees, with horror and fascination.

Ten years ago, when Cleeve retired from the Admiralty, he bought a swarm of bees. Now he has seven hives with 40,000 bees in each one, and is secretary of the Dorset Beekeepers Association.

Cleeve finds beekeeping totally absorbing. Like most people who keep bees in Britain, he does so only as a hobby as he doesn't have nearly enough bees to produce honey commercially.

Even with a veil, protective clothing and a smoker (a cylinder in which cardboard is burnt to puff smoke and pacify the bees), Cleeve has been stung countless times all over his body. He remains undeterred.

Beekeeping has proved a strenuous hobby for a retired man. Cleeve runs evening classes in the winter, looks after the 400 members of the Dorset Beekeepers Association and locates swarms for new members.

For me it is found in nature, in the relationship with one's fellows, and in the appreciation of the arts, painting, literature and above all music. With one's fellows, happiness is realized in the smile and in the eyes of those one loves, and in the effort to overcome selfishness and to seek out the best in all whom one meets.

SALE
71-73
LAURA ASHLEY
LONDON · PARIS · NEW YORK
DISPLAY DEPARTMENT

Laura Ashley

The simple, pastoral style of Laura Ashley clothes seems to reflect the quiet, simple lady who designs them. And yet, paradoxically, Laura Ashley Ltd is one of the most aggressive, successful, expanding businesses in the retail trade.

Inevitably it is assumed that because the company bears her name, it is a one-woman show. The story began in 1950 when Bernard Ashley left his job in the City to begin designing and printing modern fabrics. Laura had been working as a secretary at the National Federation of Women's Institutes in Merthyr Tydfil before she married Bernard. After the birth of the first of her four children she left her job and decided to turn to designing. Bernard taught Laura to print tablemats, napkins and tea-towels by a silk-screen process in their kitchen. Demand for the products was immediate and the Ashleys moved to Wales, where they bought a disused social club which they turned into a workshop.

To keep costs down, the firm handles every step of production from the moment the raw cotton fabric comes off the loom. It is dyed, printed, cut and sewn in Laura Ashley factories, dispatched in Laura Ashley vans to Laura Ashley shops. From its humble beginnings the business now has 2,000 employees, a turnover of £25 million and eighty shops around the world.

My best pal is my husband, he's very witty and makes me laugh a lot. When we're laughing together I feel very happy. Often when I am alone I remember things he has said and it makes me laugh all over again.

Our children like laughing, too. When we are all together in a big crowd, especially with Grandma, we can be very noisy, telling funny stories and so on. Then if we start singing and dancing, there is no end to it.

I know some people who, strictly speaking, must be described as comedians. One of them writes poetry as well – Welsh poetry, so it's difficult to understand – but never mind, he is amusing from start to finish; in fact you find tears running down your cheeks, which is how it should be.

I have always lived with very funny people, and in fact worked with them, too (they won't mind me saying so, I'm sure). I should like best of all to be a real wit myself, but my mind is just a bit too slow!

I am really very lucky, because I could die laughing.

Ann Atkin

Although she tries not to have favourites, Ann Atkin is especially fond of Siegfried, Alfred and Hierodat, three of the most likeable gnomes amongst the 700 who live on her gnome reserve.

And it seems that the gnomes like Ann – not one has tried to run away. Perhaps her popularity is due to her position as President and Founder of the British Gnomes Association. Gnomes have an instinctive pride and dignity of their ancient lineage and have long felt a lack of official recognition.

Ann is an artist by profession. She studied at the Royal Academy. But the gnomes have taken over her life and she has been busy making them comfortable on the reserve. They have a stream for fishing, a railway line and a constant stream of visitors, which is enough for any gnome. What makes gnomes happy? Human people who live in tune with nature.

It makes me happy just to think about Gnomes. It makes me happy to be making Gnomes in concrete or in pottery, or to be writing or speaking about them. For it makes me happiest when I can share Gnomes and the land in which the Gnomes live with other people. For Gnomes live in the inner earth, where the sun never rises and never sets, but always shines. A land where through the door of the heart anyone may enter regardless of whether they happen to be outwardly rich or poor, clever or stupid, old or young.

Comical, humble and happy, Gnomes are generally as brightly coloured as the gems and jewels they have about them. Every male Gnome looks very very old – perhaps as old as the earth, and simultaneously as young as a small child, while every female Gnome, being also ageless, is created with and never loses eternal beauty. All Gnomes combine the wisdom of the ages with the innocence of a child. It makes me happy to think about this for it enables me to love the whole of life. Gnomes represent a very real force in Nature. Little children with their acute imagination, can become a part of the world of Gnomes and Faeries, but as they get older the pressures of the outer technological world crowd in and it can become difficult for them to retain their visions into adult life. It makes me happy if I can bring little glimpses of the land of Gnomes, presented in tangible form, to share with children and adults, so that this vision may be a stable ingredient contained within the flux and flow of our changeable everyday world.

Alan Ayckbourn

How does this country's most successful playwright write plays? Does he start after breakfast and after a leisurely lunch, continue until tea time? Is he cautious and organized, spending weeks changing a sentence here, a comma there? None of it.

Alan Ayckbourn goes to considerable pains to make things difficult for himself. He hates the physical process of writing and only under the intense pressure of a deadline can he produce a word – let alone a play. So before he puts pen to paper he announces the dates the play will run, prints posters, sells tickets and auditions actors.

He then shuts himself up in his house, refuses to answer the phone or talk to anyone and works throughout the night. In less than a week the play is completed.

Alan lives and works in Scarborough, and as resident director of the theatre, each one of his plays is put on first there.

*Alan has written twenty-three plays, most of which have been smash hits (*The Norman Conquests, Bedroom Farce, Ten Times Table*), and at one time he had five plays running simultaneously in the West End.*

Sitting in front of an open log-fire digesting a good meal with the remains of an exquisite wine – the cat on my lap asleep, watching a Buster Keaton film with someone of the opposite sex with the same sense of humour, having just, the previous night, had a wild runaway success with a play 'they' said couldn't work – that would make me incredibly happy.

Gordon Baldwin

Gordon Baldwin is a potter whose work in ceramics has been exhibited around the world. He teaches at the Camberwell School of Arts and Crafts and at Eton College.

Even though Gordon trained as a potter his motives do not derive from methods but from modes – modes of perception and expression, often drawn from other arts, which trigger his own idea. In this context, technique is taken for granted or regarded purely as a means to a non-technical end.

It is not that it is not known
but it is difficult to make definitions
first defining the time
and then the reasons.
Happiness is experienced unquestionably
and then remembered
but nostalgia is no definition.
Events that are transporting
are not so much remembered
as repeatedly experienced
for they are not events in the sequence
of ordinary time
but stand as experience in all time;
the poet, the painter, the sculptor, the musician
make metaphors for these events.
But some are so private
and not to be defined
they are not to be dissembled
they are not sequential
nor leading on. They are
and they are of a strange chemistry.
Look at a beach rock, see it in the sun
feel its warmth and just for a moment
in all time you are the rock
somewhere in its deep inside darkness
illumined.
But what of the ordinary times
of happiness
What of them and their causes.
When one is happy no definitions
are made. No stopping to think.

Make a list of things – too trite!
And anyway the list would be wrong today.
A stream of words is not quite like
a mountain stream
It has momentum and meaning
and spins a great yarn
to be read.
The mountain stream is all action
and events
If only one could be content
with journeys
and give up all anxiety
about arrivals
all the time.
A heron hauls itself into the air
and flies
the fish leaps
and falls back
the mountain stream flows.
Yes to be all events and actions
flowing unquestionably
naturally. Yes.
And happy when it is like that
unquestionably
when?

Robin Batchelor

Ever since man could walk he has wanted to fly, but it wasn't until the hot air balloon was developed that man fulfilled his desire to become airborne. In June 1783, the Montgolfier brothers, French paper manufacturers, filled a 300lb bag, 33 feet in diameter, with smoke from a straw and wool fire and saw it rise 1,500 feet above Annonay near Lyons. In September, a relative sent up a lamb, a rooster and a duck. The animals returned unharmed, and later that year, a Frenchman made the first manned flight.

Fifty years later an Englishman flew from London to Wilburg in Germany, a distance of about 500 miles in eighteen hours, a brief period compared with the time such a trip would have taken by sailboat and horse-drawn coach. Robin Batchelor is one of around twenty professional balloonists in this country. Companies pay him to fly balloons emblazoned with advertising slogans. Some companies design their own balloons: Robertson's Jams have a balloon shaped like a golliwog; Osram, a light bulb; and the Post Office has a Buzby balloon.

It's not as simple to fly a balloon as one might imagine. It took Robin twenty hours of instruction in meteorology and navigation before he qualified as a professional pilot. At different altitudes, the wind blows in different directions, and there's no question of just taking off when the urge hits you. Weather conditions must be favourable; two or three people are needed to get a balloon airborne, and a balloonist is dependent on a retriever to follow him on the ground and pick him up however far from the planned target he may land.

But it's all worth it in the end, Robin claims, as the sensation of flying is the greatest feeling in the world. And Robin is lucky enough to get paid for doing what he loves most.

Quite naturally, I sometimes wonder about it all and try and understand why I still enjoy my heart rate increasing twofold when I am trying to land a balloon somewhere soft and grassy but at the same time trying to miss power wires (my biggest enemy), trees, greenhouses, motorways and sheep, pigs, horses and cows (who always want to lick the balloon); in fact anything on the ground that might damage, break or tear the balloon, when I finally manage to land. And it's a wonderful thing that there is always at least one beautiful lass who is a little shy, and standing back slightly, who has an expression that makes me want to lift her into the basket and fly away into the wild blue yonder . . .

I'll get my 1925 Bullnose Morris out of its garage and set off on an epic journey – and again I see the look of excitement and delight on the faces of both young and old. I once met a wonderful woman in a blizzard outside whose house my car had expired. She allowed me to rebuild my magneto on her kitchen table (with the help of her son's Meccano spanners) and then dry the thing out in her oven.

Apart from money, there are two things which make me happy – having a purpose in life and making friends.

David Bickers

There are 448 thalidomide victims in this country, and their physical handicaps vary from total loss of limbs, sight and hearing, to the loss of a thumb. They now range in age from 17 to 21 and so naturally they are contemplating their future careers just like any young adult leaving school.

David Bickers is one of the most seriously disabled thalidomides. He has no arms, but deformed buds with stiffened fingers; no legs, but feet that turn up at the bottom of his torso.

He helps run a talking magazine for the blind from his parents' house in Romford, Essex, mixing, splicing, editing, and narrating the tapes himself. Last year he screwed a camera to his wheelchair, and interviewed Prince Philip at Buckingham Palace.

He hopes somehow physical deformity could be desensitized, for it is his experience that people are intimidated by physical disfigurement, so he *frequently ends up putting people at ease.*

David Bickers has the initiative to start a worthwhile career in helping the blind. He wants to be a BBC radio announcer. One day he will be.

Michael Bond

Everyone knows Paddington Bear. Born in darkest Peru, he was found on Paddington Station with a note pinned to his duffle coat: 'Please look after this bear . . . thank you,' which his Aunt Lucy had written before she went into the Home for Retired Bears in Lima. His paws were sticky from munching marmalade and he needed a wash. The Brown family adopted him and he now lives (very happily) at number 32 Windsor Gardens.

Michael Bond, Paddington's creator, was brought up in darkest Reading. He isn't mad about marmalade, although children are always sending him jars of the stuff, so he passes them on to the more appreciative Paddington. Michael used to be a BBC cameraman. On a cold rainy December evening twenty-two years ago he saw a forlorn bear on the bottom shelf of a department store and felt sorry for it. While waiting for a bus to Paddington he created a story around the bear he had just bought.

Paddington is now a world-wide industry – his books sell in twenty-five countries and his face adorns pillowcases, pencils, towels, bath mats and his very own brand of marmalade.

Now Michael Bond is working on a serious novel and a new children's series about an armadillo called J. D. Polson.

Children laughing; the hum of distant traffic across Hyde Park in summer; being in love; having lots of work; fresh bread and cheese and wine practically anywhere in France; coming across music unexpectedly; sawing a piece of wood cleanly and neatly; the pleasure of a new notebook; smells – the smell of freshly cut grass, the smell of the Paris Métro; sharing special things; other people's happiness.

Chris Bonington

It was in 1962 that Chris Bonington led the first British ascent of the North Wall of the Eiger, perhaps one of his best-known mountaineering achievements. He has also climbed Everest, Annapurna and the Ogre Peak in the Himalayas.

Chris belittles the difficulties of mountain climbing. There are no worries on a mountain, he claims, because, insulated in your tent thousands of miles from the usual domestic problems of mortgages, money etc., there is only one thought in your head – to get to the top. Chris now lives in the Northern Fells of Cumbria with his family. If he feels energetic, he will go for a pre-lunch run up High Pike, a beautiful fell right beside his cottage; height – a mere 2,300 feet.

Happiness is like the wind. At times it blows strong and hard, and at others it is all too elusive. For me, the core of my own happiness is the presence and happiness of my wife, Wendy, and the shared development of our two children. The light froth of happiness is a family ski holiday in the Alps; the joyful exhilaration of a good day's climbing; my love and appreciation of the hills around me or the satisfaction of good food, good wine and good company.

Catherine Bramwell-Booth

About 120 years ago, when London's back streets were even less safe, and it was short odds whether you'd make it home unassaulted after dark; when the public's favourite recreation was watching hangings, the sewers were overflowing and abject poverty was the unquestioned lot, William Booth founded the Salvation Army and thundered his first command: 'Go for souls, and go for the worst.'

Today the army without guns is just as busy. Every night of the year 10,000 homeless men and women are given a bed, a hot meal and a roof to sleep under. Midnight soup-runs in towns all over the country provide a little warmth to the down-and-outers who sleep in the streets under polythene wrapping or in cardboard boxes.

In Britain alone the Salvation Army helps needy people through its 1,000 evangelistic centres, maternity homes for unwed mothers, children's homes and community centres. The 'Sally Anne' also has a missing persons service and offers rehabilitation courses for alcoholics. At Christmas a special effort is made for all the homeless, elderly, infirm and distressed. At ninety-seven, Catherine Bramwell-Booth, granddaughter of William Booth, is Commissioner of the Salvation Army, the highest rank. When Catherine started her career in the Army, she was sent to the East End to save sinners. Her knees would knock together so loudly that she had to shout her sermons.

Although she officially retired thirty-two years ago, she lectures new recruits to 'God's Army', attends fund-raising campaigns, and with her enthusiasm and energy embodies the Salvation Army motto and creed: Blood and Fire.

At ninety-seven I look back on so much happiness. We were seven, and as a child the companionship of younger brothers and sisters was an unfailing source of happiness, and later their friendship fostered happiness in all manner of circumstances.

In our home we were all happy! On one of the rare occasions when my father had time from his Salvation Army work to be with us, he was reading to the upper end of the family from *Uncle Remus* when overcome by the fun of the tale he laid the book down on his knee, put back his head and shouted with laughter in which we all joined. A moment of pure happiness as clear to me today as eighty-five years ago!

To remember the look on my mother's face when she showed us the new baby, drawing our attention to some special feature – its hand and the perfection of the tiny fingers with their minute nails – while the baby was drinking at her breast, is happiness today. To recall how as four or five of us stood watching she explained the wonderful fact that you couldn't run short of love when God's love is mingled with ours. So she could love the new baby and that would not take away any of her love for us. Oh what happiness to know there would always be enough love!

There is happiness in keeping animals. Guinea pigs were allowed on the lawn, safe in a wire enclosure, while their owners watched over them admiringly. For years a small white Persian cat was our pride and delight. Her name was Muffet. The house was never without dogs. One of the joys of being retired was for me to own one again, a small, affectionate, self-willed Yorkshire terrier. Her name was Fancy. She loved me enough to refuse food if I were absent, and on my return would dance in ecstasy uttering small sounds of welcome before rushing to devour the contents of her little bowl of food.

Everyone is born with a capacity for happiness. A baby can laugh before it can talk. Happiness can be developed so that it becomes an everyday delight and when it springs from trusting in God's love, even young children can realize this comfort, and their happiness grows.

Faith in God, His presence by His Spirit, creates an atmosphere in which happiness may spring up at any minute and sometimes change the trend of a whole day, making it a happy day. Where there is love happiness is not dependent on circumstances, but rather draws others into its own circle – and as that old ditty declares:

'The more we are together, the happier we shall be.'

One of my favourite lines in Salvation Army singing is:

'Happy they who trust in Jesus.'

Hallelujah!

Betty Box

With more than 200 documentaries and 40 films to her credit, Betty Box is one of the most prolific film producers in the country.

Betty started making films during the war. Her brother, also a film producer, had given her a job as secretary in his company. But with so many men called away, every hand was needed in the war effort at home, and the film industry played an important part. Betty's first assignment, which she was given twenty-four hours to complete, was to produce a film alerting the public to the dangers of the butterfly bomb. A second film, commissioned by the War Office, was made to discourage women chatting in the hairdresser's about their husbands' activities, where they had been sent, what they were doing.

Since then Betty has been associated with some of the best British films. Doctor in the House, Seventh Veil, A Tale of Two Cities, The Thirty-Nine Steps, *are all Betty Box productions.*

With her husband Peter Rogers, the producer of the Carry On *films, she lives in Beaconsfield, in Dirk Bogarde's old house.*

I'm blessed with an especially interesting career – producing movies – so it's easy for me to agree with those who say that happiness is most often found in work.

Movie-making has to be a shared experience. Happiness is far stronger – in fact for me almost only exists when shared with others; the high-spots, the sudden magic moment, even the inevitable disappointments. Giving is as great or perhaps even greater a happiness than receiving. I think millions have sung – 'I want to be happy but I can't be happy till I've made you happy too.' (Noel Coward spoke from the heart when in *Private Lives* he mentioned the 'potency of cheap music'.)

I am reminded of my first visit to Venice, when a friend insisted we wait until dusk before going into the huge Square of St Mark's, once described as 'Europe's largest drawing room'. At dusk it suddenly becomes a magic fairyland as the myriad lamps are lit and floodlights transform the cathedral face with its golden horses.

My best happinesses are visual. And there's the added happiness of looking back and remembering these things. Thank you for giving me that pleasure.

The Oxford English Dictionary *is the standard authoritative historical dictionary of the English language. First published between 1884 and 1928, it contains nearly half a million words, covering 1,200 years of the spoken and written word. Consider that the vocabulary of an averagely educated person is around 5,000 words.*

Under the aegis of Dr Robert Burchfield, the current chief editor of the Oxford dictionaries, a 70,000 word four-volume Supplement to the OED *is being produced now to update the changing English language.*

A team of researchers read every novel, poem, magazine, trade, medical and scientific journal, as well as thousands of other books, systematically collecting evidence of changing or new words.

Writers are always coining new words. P. G. Wodehouse invented many expressions which are now in common usage, and even Enid Blyton, whose books many libraries refused to stock, added the word 'parp' (of a car's horn). 'Shuttle diplomacy', 'to go bananas', 'bionic', 'microchip', are all words introduced into the language in the past few years.

Monitoring the English language is a huge and laborious undertaking. But for twenty-three years, New Zealand-born Robert has been working on what he considers the most absorbing of projects.

The English word 'happiness' came into being in the sixteenth century and was a newish word to Shakespeare and Spenser, but the idea of happiness reaches back into antiquity. 'Philosophers differ about the chief good or happiness of man,' said Sir William Temple. No doubt philosophers differ about the chief aspects of everything. My own pursuit of happiness has turned out to lie in the pursuit of excellence in areas of life where my own physical or mental powers allowed it.

The Oxford dictionaries to which I have contributed make up my lexicographical pleasure garden. A dictionary, like a novel, has a plot, and the plot is the property of the editor. Its development and enrichment is governed by those who work with him.

Private pleasures are also listable; among them, driving into Oxford each day, city of words; trig-point spotting (I was a surveyor in the army); Schubert's 'Trout'; the red berries of my cotoneaster and my ivy-cleared hedges; *The Times*, Drambuie, and sausages with herbs from a small family butcher in the Oxford covered market.

Dr Robert Burchfield

Barbara Cartland

Happiness is love. When we give and receive love we know a happiness which makes us look beautiful, and we find the whole world around us is transformed.

Everyone who falls in love says:

'This is different,' and it *is* different from the ordinary, mundane feelings we knew before love changed them.

Love begins with a man and woman, goes on to their children, and is what mankind has sought since the beginning of creation in something higher, better and finer than himself which he calls God.

Barbara Cartland, is a writer, an historian, a playwright and political speaker. One of the most prolific authors of our time, she has written over 280 books. She has beaten the world record for the last four years by writing 21, 24, 20 and 23 books; 110 million copies of these have been published throughout the world. Her novels are dictated between one o'clock and three-thirty when she has completed between six and seven thousand words. Her heroines never go to bed with the hero until they are married and the Barbara Cartland concept of love is that it is both spiritual and physical and is the ideal that all men and women seek in their hearts.

Barbara Cartland, who is seventy-eight, has many other interests. She is president of the National Association of Health, the founder and owner of the only Romany gypsy camp in the world, and president of the Hertfordshire branch of the Royal College of Midwives. She has recorded an Album of Love Songs, *with the Royal Philharmonic Orchestra, and continues to write her novels at the rate of one every two weeks. She is also a well-known television personality and her novel* The Flame is Love *has been shown on NBC in the United States, and will shortly be seen in Britain, Japan, Australia, Canada and other countries.*

Kim Casali

Kim Casali is the originator of the 'Love is . . .' cartoons. Syndicated by the Los Angeles Times *to newspapers in sixty countries, her cartoon strip could be one of the most popular in history. And if that's not enough 'Love is . . .' for you, there are countless items to buy for your loved one, from calendars to keyrings, aprons, clocks, mugs, soap, cosmetics, stationery or towels.*

The LA Times *sends Kim a list of possible captions, and she bases her drawings on them. It takes her about half an hour to draw a cartoon, and she works four to five months in advance.*

Kim was born in New Zealand. She trained as a nurse, but decided in her early twenties to start a new life in America. She took a succession of jobs, and while working as a receptionist at an advertising company, where time hung heavily, Kim started to doodle the Love figures. Customers of the firm would ask if they could buy them which encouraged Kim to send them to a newspaper.

For a woman so associated with love, Kim has undergone a lot of sadness. Her father died when she was four, and a brother was hit by a car in front of her home. Her husband, Robert, died lingeringly of cancer a few years ago. But Kim, ever an optimist, decided to have his sperm deep-frozen so that she could have a child by artificial insemination. Milo was born sixteen months after his father had died.

'Love is the pursuit of happiness'

With my romantic nature, being in love makes me happy, ecstatically happy.

The happiness that sustains me is provided by my children. Each phase they go through is delightful to me. They bring me untold pleasure by just sharing my life.

Many, many things give me fleeting moments of happiness, like a robin accompanying me while I work in the garden.

If I am depressed and need some instant happiness I can get that quite easily by watching a good comedy at the cinema or by taking a drive with a handful of cassettes of my favourite music. I get guaranteed happiness from the sun. Let the sun shine and I shine, especially if the temperature is very warm.

Sir Hugh Casson

Sir Hugh Casson has designed such diverse projects as the Elephant House at the London Zoo and the interior of the royal yacht Britannia. *He is now president of the Royal Academy of Arts, founded in 1768, which is the oldest established society in Great Britain solely devoted to the fine arts.*

It is undoubtedly through its exhibitions that the Academy has become best known in the world. The Summer Exhibition of contemporary paintings, drawings, engravings, sculpture and architecture, has been held annually without a break for over two hundred years. Some 10,000 works by 4,000 artists of all nationalities are submitted, and of those, about 1,300 are finally chosen. It is a unique chance for an artist to become well known.

Happiness for me demands every day three ingredients – not in order of importance, nor as easy to find as they sound.

First a daily – if tiny – success, be it no more than finding a taxi on a wet night, or a book that you want in stock. Secondly – a daily hug – real or metaphorical, to make you feel wanted. Thirdly – a daily glimpse of the horizon – be it no wider than the sky at the end of the street.

If these ingredients are to be fully enjoyed they must be constantly stirred by curiosity; for it is curiosity which expands our experience and which teaches us to recognize beauty, and thus ultimately to command happiness.

Unless you're accustomed to spending a great deal of time with the Queen, it's an unnerving experience meeting Jeannette. One feels constantly disoriented as she speaks of her three children, husband Kenneth and detached house in suburban Essex.

Surprisingly, it didn't occur to Jeannette until she was sixteen that she resembled the then Princess Elizabeth. It was on a boat trip to Holland with her parents and younger sister. As she disembarked, a cheering, shouting crowd gathered to greet her on the dock. Jeannette blushed and didn't know where to look.

Now Jeannette makes a living out of her resemblance to the Monarch. She is paid to mingle at cocktail parties, read annual reports, present awards and open shopping centres. She is a staunch royalist so she carefully vets any functions that are of the slightest potential impropriety.

Jeannette studies the Queen's gestures, voice and mannerisms on a video cassette recorder. By another strange coincidence, Jeannette has had to start wearing glasses in the past few years.

My first remembrance of an overwhelming feeling of happiness was when I had passed the eleven-plus exam and achieved a place in Wembley High School.

Happiness came to me again when I met my husband. I had emigrated to America after acting in repertory for years and getting nowhere; my husband, an oilman, had come to Midland, Texas, to meet the heads of oil companies that he would be talking to once he took up the position of drilling manager for an oil company in Canada. I was on cloud nine.

Experiencing the wonder of conceiving my first baby gave me an unbelievable happiness that I truly feel could never have the same impact. The wonder and joy of producing life within your own body can never come twice. At last you actually have the knowledge of what you previously could only imagine.

When I have finished my act before an audience, if the applause is overwhelming – then I am truly happy.

I put a ten-cent piece into a slot machine in Las Vegas in 1978, and the bells started to ring and the machine shook to life; the thrill was of a happiness, a childish excitement. Guards surrounded me and everyone looked, I was so happy that I stayed at the machines for hours and I won two more jackpots, ending up with more than 500 dollars. I can't wait to return to Las Vegas and the slot machines.

JEANNETTE CHARLES

Tommy Clitheroe

The essential requirements for a successful children's holiday by the sea are an unlimited amount of sweets, an extra pound or so pocket money, and a ride on a donkey.

And on Blackpool's golden sands, right under the Tower, Tommy Clitheroe has ten donkeys which for fifteen pence any child (under six stone) can ride. There's Ann and Gigi, Jimmy and Prince, Simon and Sonny, Jackie, Jenny, Eeyore and Misty. Tommy knows them all by name and talks to them like favourite dogs.

Sometimes a donkey gets carried away and Tommy will have to run all over the sands to retrieve an exhilarated child who realizes he's getting more than his money's worth.

The season lasts from Whitsun to the end of October and when the last illumination is extinguished on the famous promenade, the donkeys go to a farm, and Tommy looks for work as a slater until the next year.

A grand in me pocket, out with me mates having a bevvy. I'm happy when the sun shines and I make plenty of money on the beach. I'm happy when the donkeys don't die at spring of year. I'm happy when I know my family is OK. You have to like kids when you work on the beach so I'm happy when I see how happy the kids are on the donkeys.

George Cooke

George Cooke has a staff of 150 gardeners and 2,000 acres. He's the superintendent of the Royal Parks and Gardens at Hampton Court, responsible for maintaining part of our precious heritage. Under his aegis a 220 year old vine still produces 700 lb of grapes a year, deer roam Bushey Park as they did when Henry VIII took the palace from Cardinal Wolsey, and visitors continue to get lost in the maze. George was brought up in the Vale of Esk and worked on the Duke of Gloucester's estate. From there he studied for a degree at the Royal Horticultural School in Wisley and then was appointed to his present job six years ago.

Being a Welshman and a former rugby player, I get great pleasure watching rugby at international level when the Welsh team is involved. In recent years their achievements have been superb and when I see the red jerseys sported by the Welsh team, this makes me feel extremely happy.

I find reading relaxing; I get so engrossed that I cannot stop until the end of the book.

What can be more pleasant than sitting with a rod on the bank of a river or stream in the heart of the countryside waiting for the unexpected to happen? Whatever happens, I'm very happy indeed.

Last but not least, I get great contentment from having a nap after a satisfying lunch at weekends and this gives me a feeling of freedom from any problems or responsibilities.

Jilly Cooper

Jilly Cooper has been sacked from dozens of jobs. As a very temporary secretary, receptionist, copywriter and account executive, she was a devastatingly bad employee, never on a payroll more than a few months because of her inefficiency, bad timekeeping and vagueness. Now Jilly has a great wealth of material to draw on for her books and articles.

Her first attempt at a novel (about show-jumping) never saw the light of day. She left the 50,000 word manuscript on a bus, and it was never returned.

For twelve years, Jilly has had a column on the Sunday Times. *Before that she was editor of a teenage magazine where the ideas for her series of romantic novels originated: sweet young things falling for successful, handsome, hard-hearted plutocrats who are won over in the end.*

Discipline for a writer is essential. Jilly works from nine to seven, typing out her stories as she can't read her handwriting. Sometimes it takes fifteen drafts before she's satisfied.

Inspiration is drawn from her home surroundings. Daughter Emily once made a remark that found its way into a novel: 'You may not be very clever, Mummy, but at least you're good at mopping up sick.' Husband Leo has been revealed to the world often enough, and now Jilly's two dogs, Mabel Mongrel and Fortnum, are about to be immortalized in a new book.

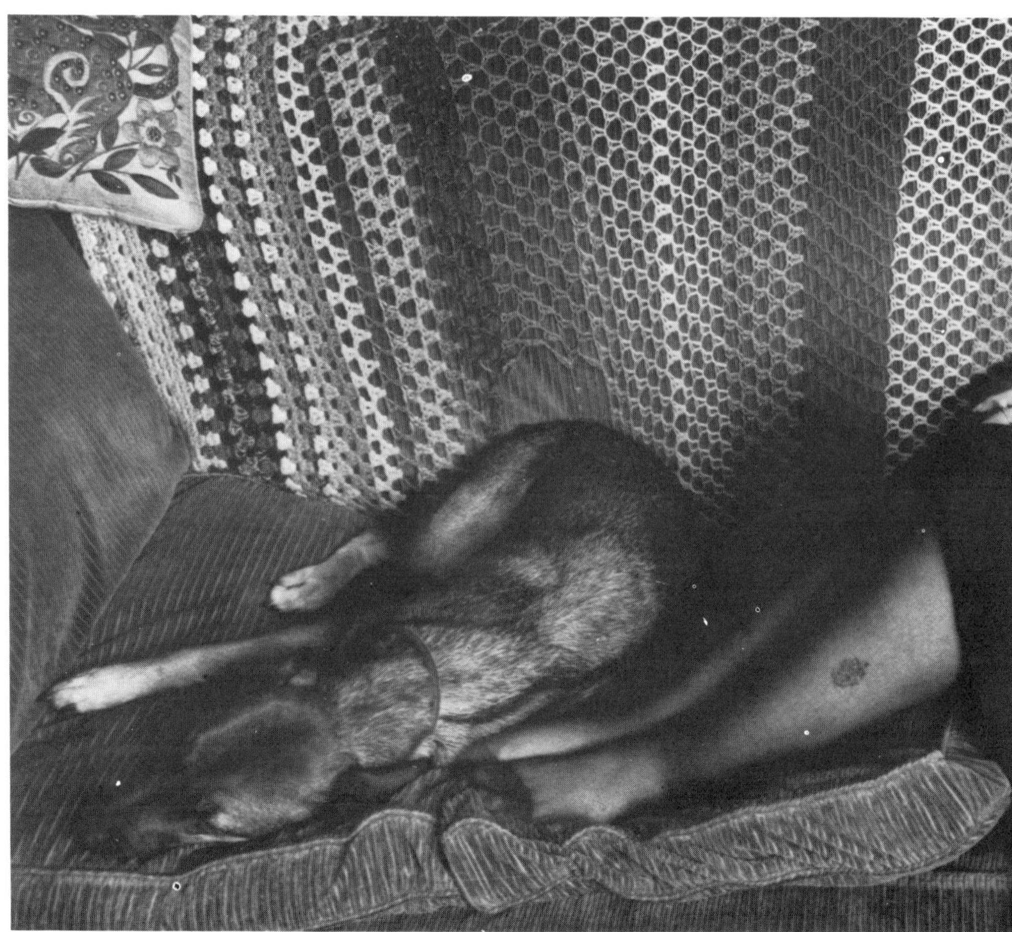

I think what makes me happy is the right balance of work and play, of company and solitude, of enough achievement to be able to feel you can fool around for a day or so. My husband, my parents and my children bring me intense happiness, so do my dogs and walking them in the country. I love carousing with my friends, I love being alone with a good book or a good idea. I love eating, drinking and making love. I love music and walking around my garden in bare feet at dawn, seeing what new flowers have opened in the night. I love writing 'THE END' when I've finished a piece or even better a book. I like having a good giggle almost best of all.

15
Butlin's
MINEHEAD
1ST
Butlin's
MINEHEAD
3RD

Brett Cresswell believes in entertaining on a large scale. He has over ten thousand visitors at a time, and 250,000 in a season.

Brett is entertainment director at Butlin's in Minehead. He's the man who organizes the fun, and you can place direct responsibility for the success or failure of your holiday on his shoulders. He certainly thinks up a lot of amusements for all age groups. The grandmothers competition (Glam Grans) is a popular event, so is Singalong Time, Bingo, crazy golf, ballroom dancing, trampolining, roller skating, whist drives, and a competition called Miss Che Che to find the most cheerful and chubby lady in the camp.

Brett's first job was as a redcoat in 1955, and his whole life has revolved around Butlin's. He even met his wife who was a disc jockey for Radio Butlin's at the Skegness camp.

There have been many changes over the years at Butlin's, Brett says. Now seventy per cent of the guests cater for themselves, and the entertainment is more sophisticated. Discos, pinball machines and all the fun of the fair. And perhaps most dramatic change of all, there is no longer a wakey wakey call bright and early in the morning.

Brett Cresswell

Being a Butlin entertainment manager, it is my pleasurable task to dispense 'instant happiness' to thousands of our holidaymakers. In consequence, I become saturated in a sort of reflected happiness. This may not be true happiness but if my work occupies half of my waking hours, then I am halfway to being a happy person. I feel that luck or good fortune may contribute significantly towards happiness.

Happiness is caring and sharing. The other half of my waking hours is well taken care of; this idyllic state is brought about by being married to Brenda. She would top a long list of things which keep me happy; things such as:

Holidays
Animals
Portugal
Pictures
Illusionists (I used to be one)
Nuits St George
Escargot
Sinatra
Sunshine

but happiness is nothing if not shared.

There are few sounds more profoundly moving than a Welsh male voice choir in full song. And the village of Treorchy in the heart of the Rhondda valley boasts one of the finest choirs in all of Wales. Men from all professions get together three times a week in the hall of the local primary school to rehearse a repertoire of more than 700 songs which they perform publicly in about thirty performances a year, for no more reward than the pure love of singing.

John Cynan Jones is the conductor of the choir as well as deputy headmaster of the local comprehensive. He says the key word to being a good conductor is communication, and the good-natured rapport between him and 'the lads' is obvious, even when he's ticking off the bass section for missing a beat.

As representatives of Wales, the Treorchy male choir are incomparable ambassadors. There are 118 men in the choir, ranging in age from 18 to 87, and with songs like 'The March of the Men of Harlech', 'Sospan Fach', 'Yr Arglwydd yw fy Mugail' (The Lord is my Shepherd) or even showbusiness numbers like 'The Impossible Dream', they can stir the heart, produce laughter or move to tears.

JOHN CYNAN JONES

Like many Welshmen, my main sources of happiness are rugby, music and family. In my case all three are fused together, since my wife, daughter and two sons are equally fanatical rugby supporters and are naturally musical. Both my sons and I sing with the choir at the beautiful cathedral at Brecon, and the whole family are members of the choir at our local village church.

To a Welshman the game of rugby football is the greatest sport in all the world, and the sight of one's own wing three-quarter crossing the opponents' try-line (especially if it be England's!) gives one a rich glow of satisfaction similar to that experienced after consuming a bottle of good wine.

Our concerts normally encompass the whole gamut of emotion, giving rise to many moments of pure magic, which produce in me an ecstasy of happiness, making me realize I am probably the most fortunate musician in the whole world!

WHILE shepherds watched their flocks by night,
All seated on the ground,
The angel of the Lord came down,
And glory shone around.
"Fear not," said he; for mighty dread
Had seized their troubled mind;
"Glad tidings of great joy I bring
To you and all mankind.
"To you in David's town this day
Is born of David's line
A Saviour Who is Christ the Lord;
And this shall be the sign;
"The heavenly babe you there shall find
To human view displayed,
All meanly wrapped in swathing bands,
And in a manger laid."
Thus spake the seraph; and forthwith
Appeared a shining throng
Of angels praising God, who thus
Addressed their joyful song:
glory be to God on high,
to the earth be peace;
will henceforth from heaven to men
Begin and never cease."

John Darwin

The Palace of Westminster occupies the site of the old royal palace which was the chief residence of the kings from Canute to Henry VIII. Now it is the workplace of 630 members of parliament and a thousand or so peers of the realm.

Responsibility for running this huge conglomeration of buildings falls on John Darwin, the resident engineer. He looks after the heating, lighting, works of art and even the structure of the Palace.

As a qualified engineer John has designed wind-tunnels, heat chambers, airfields and ships. He took on his current job after retiring from the Department of the Environment, and finds the increased workload at the age of sixty-five enormously stimulating.

We photographed John from the inside of Big Ben at exactly eleven a.m. (You don't easily forget the sound of an hour bell weighing 16½ tons ringing eleven times six yards away from your ear.) The chimes are traditionally associated with the lines 'Lord, through this hour, Be thou our guide, That by Thy power, No foot shall slide.' Try humming it next time you pass Big Ben on the hour.

There is no disguising the happy glow that comes from the early-morning sun gilding the hundreds of pinnacles of this most beautiful Palace of Westminster which I can see from my bedroom; suddenly appearing through the Gothic tracery of our stone mullioned windows or the sound of the great bells flying from the floodlit glory of Big Ben. These joys only become real happiness, however, when they are shared with some kindred spirit. Indeed the only true happiness is that which is reflected back from the eyes of all those with whom one has shared some part of the enjoyment of life.

Happiness should be a by-product of a busy healthy life with help and consideration of other people.

And after the problems of the day what joy to relax in a hot bath reading poetry aloud. Among poems I often quote to myself are those from R. L. Stevenson:

If I have faltered more or less
In my great task of happiness;
If I have moved among my race
And shown no glorious morning face;
If beams from happy human eyes
Have moved me not; if morning skies
Books, and my food and summer rain
Knocked on my sullen heart in vain:
Lord, thy most pointed pleasure take
And stab my spirit broad awake.

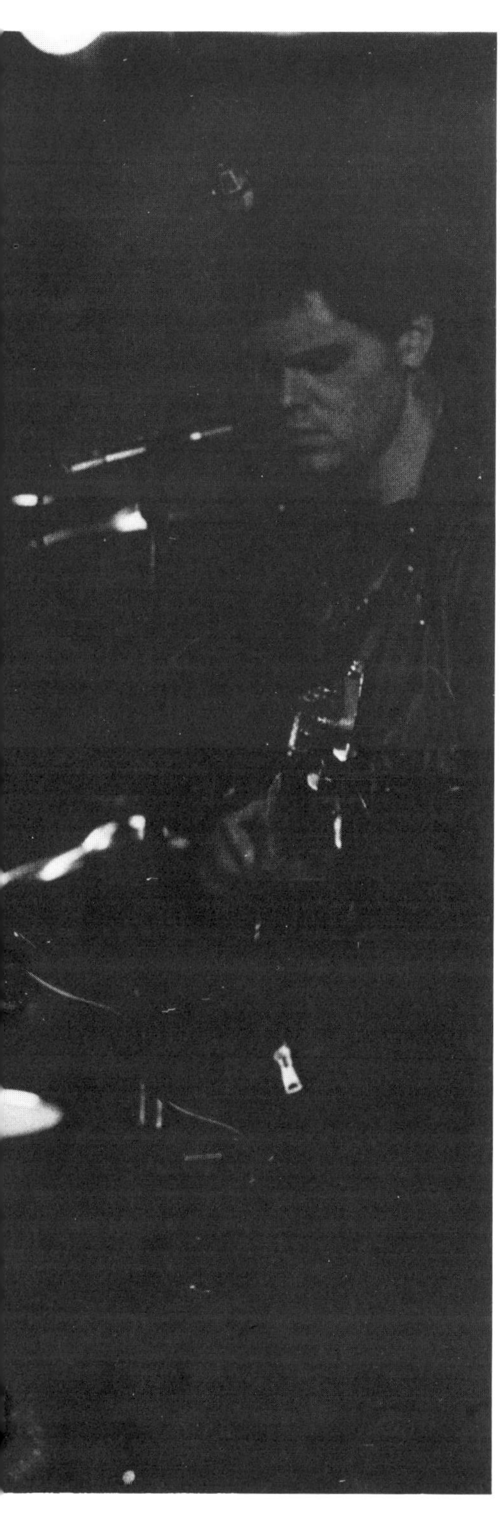

Tony Doughty

Tony Doughty, 21, grew up in Crawley, went to the local comprehensive where he got eleven O-levels and two A-levels, won a fencing medal for England in the under-sixteen internationals, and should, he admits, have gone on to university. But he went to London and joined a pop group, and as time got longer, thoughts of further education faded.

He has played with a lot of bands. He changed his name to Stretch Armstrong and joined up with Peroxide Romance. For a short time he fronted a punk band and then played bass guitar with Eddy and the Hot Rods. As lead singer of the Outpatients, Stretch became interested in theatrical rock, and would be carried on stage in a coffin from where he would sing his first number.

Stretch is now lead singer of Agent Orange which used to be the X-Ray Specs before Poly Styrene left. They're making a demo tape and hopes are high. Stretch is learning to read and write music.

The big problem is money. Clubs pay less than £20 for an unknown group to play for an hour. Still, although Stretch admits that he's completely broke, he is confident that with Agent Orange his big break is just around the corner.

Being rather a strange person, I obtain happiness from the most unlikely of sources, an example of which happened this morning. An old lady burdened down with groceries (a dozen eggs and a few bits and bobs which seemed to account for that week's pension) fell over in the street a few yards in front of me. One 'gentleman' preferred not to see this while another stood a good twenty feet away and shouted, 'You all right, dear?' (A common policy adopted by many.) I stepped in and helped her up to her feet and she was so thankful. 'Thank you, young man, you are a gentleman.' I kept quiet about being a musician. I felt so happy and thought about mugging her but seeing most of her pension smashed on the floor, decided against it.

No, for my excitement I just enjoy the thrill of performing. There are no words to express the kick I get from it. To have people watching you perform, whether they number one or one hundred thousand, is just fabulous. Musical rewards are rarely financial. (I don't have twelve Rolls-Royces, half a dozen assorted sports cars or various luxury apartments around the world.) I have never enjoyed the luxury of money. The average lifespan of most musicians when they do make it is usually only about three years. The only aim I have is to be happy, and to make other people happy, and if this means accepting the insecurities that are involved in my line of work then I am prepared to accept them for many years to come.

Of course drugs, drink, and teenage sex orgies always help to break the monotony . . .

Roy Duval

With all his clothes on, Roy Duval looks of average height and build. You can't tell that all his clothes have to be specially made. But stripped to a pair of shorts, there is no hiding the awesome physique that has won him the titles of Mr Britain, Mr Europe, Mr World and Mr Universe.

Bodybuilding is an increasingly popular sport in Britain, in fact after America we are considered the best in the world. Aficionados *liken the bodybuilder to a sculptor who works on his body instead of stone. Objectives are size, definition and quality of muscle, plus bulk combined with overall symmetry, power and grace. A panel of judges decides who wins a tournament using these criteria.*

At thirty-four, Roy has been training for fifteen years, eating a regular low-carbohydrate, high-protein diet, and lifting weights two hours a day, six days a week. As manager of a health club in Trowbridge, he has easy access to all the facilities he needs.

By the time he's forty, Roy thinks he'll be approaching the peak of his form. Until then, there's little chance of his getting sand kicked in his face.

When Roy stops winning awards, he'll give up his rigorous training-schedule, and let his muscles shrink back to their regular size.

As a competitive bodybuilder any physical progress I make will give me a lot of happiness. But what makes me really happy is when I go to the gym and see so many others, from all walks of life, training and trying to improve their health and physical appearance.

H. J. Eysenck

Professor Hans Eysenck is no stranger to controversy. Whatever he says seems to land him in hot water. Through his belief that IQ (intelligence quotient) is a hereditary characteristic, he has claimed that American blacks are less intelligent than American whites, Irishmen somewhat less intelligent than Englishmen, and Orientals more clever than Caucasians, and consequently managed to insult pretty much the whole human race.

His views on any given subject are naturally unconventional. Take astrology – he has found a relationship between star signs and personality traits. He suggests the use of drugs for the rehabilitation of criminals and has just written a book which debunks the theory that smoking is bad for the health.

Happiness as an ecstatic state of being is of course very rare in the lives of most people; I recall a few occasions, as when I won my first tennis tournament, kissed my first girl, saw for the first time the numerical result of an experiment come out in line with my hypothesis, or went off on holiday with the woman I loved.

A milder state of happiness is perhaps more frequent, and can be maintained for a long period of time. It depends on a person's continuing health, satisfactory work adjustment, happy marital relations, nice children, achievements commensurate with ambitions, and perhaps most of all a happy temperament – which, being largely inherited, is difficult to ensure by any manipulation of the environment! Having lived in such a continuing state of happiness for the last thirty years, I can recommend it.

Reverend Mother Sister Edna Francis

A typical day at the Convent of St John the Baptist in Windsor would go like this:

6.00 a.m.	*Rising Bell*
6.45	*Lauds*
7.00	*Mass*
7.30	*Breakfast*
8.30–9.30	*Mental prayers*
9.30	*Tierce*
10.00	*Work around the Convent*
12.00	*Sext*
1.00 p.m.	*Lunch*
1.30	*None*
2.00	*Free time*
3.00–4.30	*More work*
4.30	*Tea*
5.00	*Spiritual Reading*
5.30	*Vespers*
6.30	*Work*
7.30	*Supper*
8.30	*Prayer*
9.45	*Compline*
10.00	*Lights out*

The Reverend Mother Superior of the Convent, Sister Edna Francis is sixty-three. She has been an Anglican nun for twenty-one years and was elected Reverend Mother six years ago. She used to work on her father's farm in Cambridgeshire. She is in charge of around forty nuns, ranging in age from 22 to 91.

'Our hearts are restless until they find their rest in thee.' So wrote St Augustine; for him as for many people, happy are those who know their need of God.

To need God. . . God is infinite, but one in whom we put our whole trust and who is loving, caring and steadfast amid the chaos of our lives. To be at one with the power behind the universe allows happiness to blossom, and love, joy and peace are the fruit, and suddenly there is beauty everywhere – in a raindrop, a rosebud, a pot plant, a baby, an old man's lined face or a woman's work-worn hand, the sun on bricks – the list is endless.

DISTILLERY
ROAD

It is said there are two things a Scotsman likes naked and one of them is women. The other one, in case you haven't guessed, is one of Scotland's most revered products – malt whisky.

Ian Fyfe is assistant manager of the Glengarioch Distillery in Oldmeldrum, Aberdeenshire. Twenty-three years ago, Ian started at the distillery as a lofter – the lowest position in the whole manufacture of whisky – stirring the barley in the loft to get air into it.

Married, with two daughters, he is now a 'granda'. For perfect health, Ian says, he takes three neat glasses of whisky a day.

Ian Fyfe

Moments of simple pleasure begin at five-thirty a.m. when I make my rounds of the still and have a talk with each of the three members of the night shift. To me a distillery is a living thing, working night and day. On a fine summer morning there can be no greater uplift than to watch the sun rising slowly in the east. No matter what problems the coming day will bring, I am nearly always in a happy frame of mind when the day shift yokes for work at seven a.m.

In spite of the snow and the coarse weather, winter brings its social compensations. During days of 'bleen drift', we stand around the coke-fired stove in the cooperage which Sid has just stoked up until it's 'reel het'. Feeling comfortable and secure and happily sheltered from the harsh weather, we start yarning away to one another like a lot of old sailors in a dockside tavern. We talk about the village characters and recount all the hilarious stories surrounding them. We've heard them all before like the time drunk Bob locked himself in the wardrobe and thinking all the time he was in the lavatory. With a dram or two inside us we laugh until our bellies ache.

If I take a liking to a party of visitors to the distillery and I think they are deserving of another dram, I'll give it to them. With no inhibitions holding them back and with me egging them on, they'll sing, recite, tell stories, dance and really enjoy themselves. It is fine to make other people happy.

Whisky is a great stimulant for bringing the best out of people!

Sandy Gall

Playing a round of golf at Rye, or on some other seaside course, particularly in the spring when the larks are singing, with friends, and preferably winning: having a large glass of gin afterwards and some lunch and going out again in the afternoon with the sun on my back and the sea blue across the dunes, and completing another eighteen holes, with a few pars and a couple of birdies and not even minding not winning!

It's long been a tradition at ITN that all the newscasters are trained journalists and write many of the bulletins themselves.

Sandy Gall joined ITN in 1963 and is currently an anchorman on News at Ten. *He arrives at the London studio at three p.m. and usually writes the bongs (the nickname for the headline items read between Big Ben's chimes) and two or three feature stories himself.*

Sandy was born in Malaya where his father was a rubber planter. After leaving Aberdeen University, where he read French and German, he joined Reuters as a trainee foreign correspondent. His first posting was to Germany, where the first story he was told to cover was never filed, he moved so slowly. Fortunately his skills as a journalist improved and in two years he was covering the whole of East Africa. Life was very exciting and dangerous for a foreign correspondent. In 1972 Sandy got slung into a Ugandan jail by Idi Amin (his deportation papers have pride of place in the downstairs loo), and the experience inspired him to write his first novel.

The television companies have always believed it too distracting for newscasters to become personalities and they are advised to keep low profiles. But inevitably with only three television channels a newscaster's face becomes familiar, and Sandy is always recognized on the streets.

Sandy lives in a fifteenth-century low-beamed cottage in Kent. For viewers who are interested, he's married with four children, six feet two inches tall and 53 years old.

Alfred William John Gooding

Alfred William John Gooding is a dirty old man. He's a chimney sweep, and by the time he's cleaned his first chimney at five-thirty in the morning he's covered head to toe in soot.

For thirty-four years Fred's been sweeping the chimneys of London, and has never taken a holiday. I couldn't resist asking him if he dances on the roof tops. None of it – he hates heights. He does like dog racing, and in the afternoon, when his day is done, Fred is invariably to be found at the tracks. (A curious London ordinance says that sweeps must finish their working day at noon.)

It will cost you a fiver to procure the services of A. W. J. Gooding. His brooms will clean a chimney of eighty feet – if it's higher than that he has to drop a ball and chain from the roof.

One service which Fred performs for free is officiating at weddings. Tradition has it that a chimney sweep (with brooms and topper) will bring newlyweds happiness and prosperity. And then, of course, and this is the bit Fred likes, the bride must kiss the sweep.

You only need three things in life to make you happy. Your health; enough work to keep you out of mischief; and a bit of the other.

'With eye upraised, his master's look to scan,
The joy, the solace, and the aid of man;
The rich man's guardian and the poor man's friend,
The only creature faithful to the end.'

BYRON

Michael Graver

The Battersea Dogs Home is a paradox. It's supported and financed by dog lovers – but it wouldn't exist if people were more caring.

Last year the Dogs Home took in 16,000 lost or starving dogs and 1,000 stray cats. Of that number 3,500 were reclaimed by owners, and almost 8,000 were sold. 5,500 had to be put down – electrocuted.

Michael Graver has been a keeper at the home for ten years. He thinks people are very irresponsible. They buy a puppy but don't think through the consequences. A dog needs as much care as a child.

My life is divided between the hours I spend working at the Dogs Home and the time which I spend with my family at home. I am one of those fortunate beings who obtains great happiness not only from my domestic life, but also from my work. I also enjoy watching competitive sport such as football, cricket and tennis.

What gives me great pleasure and happiness is arriving at the home early in the morning and being greeted by the animals who are always delighted when the staff turn up for work.

There are moments of great joy. Such as, when one is taking a distressed owner of a dog around the home to see if his lost animal is there. After peering into kennel after kennel and shaking his head, when the owner finally comes to the kennel where his dog is resting and discovers the long-lost pet there is a moment of sheer happiness, not only for the two of them, but also for the keeper who has helped to reunite them. No less the sense of happiness which one feels when one sees a sick animal recover after a long illness or injury or when a visitor decides to give a new home to one of the deserted animals. As the visitor is sizing up the animal, so the animal is sizing up the new owner and obviously saying to itself, 'I hope he does not desert me as the last one did.' Each day we wave off the premises happy dogs going off with their happy owners and hope that they will have a happy new life together.

Ron Gunn

A good sound recordist needs strong arms to hold up a microphone for indeterminate lengths of time; good ears to orchestrate sound tones and levels, and the aggression to push himself through journalists and cameramen so that he can be nearest to whoever is in the public eye.

According to Ron Gunn the hardest assignments are accompanying royal events, because it's not allowed to record unscripted royal conversation, so if he's on a live broadcast, he must be quick not *to catch any royal asides.*

As an employee of Yorkshire Television, Ron can be whisked off at a moment's notice. He accompanied Alan Whicker on a millionaire's cruise to Palm Beach, spent three months in India, and a gruesome fortnight in a Dallas emergency hospital unit which dealt with killings, knifings and muggings every evening.

Even in these days of advanced camera and video equipment, a passing aeroplane or car can drown out an important interview. When we met up with Ron at Stonehenge, his recording of the Druid chants was drowned by a helicopter – hired by his own company.

If I can make someone happy, then I'm happy. Bringing presents back from overseas for the family. Searching for that little something different that you can't get at home and then to see the look of anticipation and excitement on the faces of the children (three teenagers now) before I open my suitcase – it's like Christmas morning.

For self-indulged happiness, Sunday, with papers in the morning, a couple of pints before a home-made Sunday lunch, falling asleep afterwards in the chair in front of the telly, sheer bliss!

To share a good laugh with someone, telling a joke to friends or hearing a joke for the first time when it's told well with feeling for the story line.

Jeanette Hartley

Jeanette Hartley travels only by Concorde. As a stewardess for British Airways, Jeanette has been making four or five round trips a month to New York, to Washington and to Bahrain for the past three years.

Stewardesses apply to work on Concorde, and as there are only six BA Concordes in service at the moment, competition for a place is fierce among the 2,800 stewardesses.

There is no doubt that Concorde is a pioneer in a new era of aviation history. It is the first commercial aircraft to travel at supersonic speeds, and it flies at 1,320 m.p.h. (faster than a bullet, twice the speed of sound), which effectively halves the time of transatlantic flights. On board, Concorde pampers the 100 passengers it can accommodate with lashings of caviare and buckets of champagne. Mind you, with a £650 one-way ticket to New York, cocoa and a digestive biscuit would seem a little stingy.

What does a jetsetter do when she's not jetsetting? Jeanette is a communications Wren in the Reserve, and at her cottage in the village of Wexham near Slough, her favourite playmate is her nine-year-old horse, Muschamp Prattel.

Having the gifts of life and good health. We should do our best to help and serve other people and follow the Christian principles: only in this way can we lead a genuinely fulfilling and happy life. I believe, too, that one should never expect too much out of life but be thankful for the good things that happen. Life is what we make it, the world owes us nothing, and happiness, like everything else, has to be worked at.

During one of my visits to the United States I remember seeing in a card shop somewhere the words of an American philosopher on happiness, and they will always stick in my mind. His recipe for a happy life contained three very simple, basic ingredients: something to do, someone to love, and something to hope for. And I believe if we can forget about ourselves and do our best for other people then it is possible to have a really happy life.

Alistair Henderson

On the northern tip of the most northern island of the Outer Hebrides stands the Butt of Lewis Lighthouse. It's the first major landfall from Canada.

The lighthouse was built almost 120 years ago by Robert Louis Stevenson's father and stands 170 feet above sea level. On a clear day you can see forty miles out to sea.

Alistair Henderson has been a lighthouse keeper for six years now. His family live in a tied cottage beside the lighthouse and as there are two other men to share the twenty-four-hour service, he sees plenty of them.

Alistair used to be a rat-catcher in Glasgow, but now he feels he has found his true vocation. His eyes shine as he talks about non-directional radio beacons and the electronic paraphernalia the modern lighthouse keeper must master.

First, good health; second, a fine family; third, a job I enjoy doing; and fourth, my hobbies, in which I have time to indulge, thanks to my job.

A lighthouse is a good place to bring up a family; there's no real comparison with the environment the boys would have had if we were living in the city. Life seems so much more personal, far less frantic, people have more time for each other.

I think that my only regret is not finding this job years ago!

Holmwood School

Holmwood School is a preparatory and kindergarten school for girls and boys aged 4–9 years old in Salisbury. Mrs Lewin is the Headmistress. From left to right in the photograph:

Alasdair Maclay I like going to the circus. I like reading books. I like going to Justin's house because he is my best friend. I like our lane – because it has new tarmac and my bike goes faster than ever and it bumps.

Amanda Claydon I like reading books of fairy tales with happy endings. I love to help my little brother to swim because he likes that and we can go in the big paddling pool without Mummy.

Jonathan Chalke I like playing with my toys most of all my panda and my squirrel. They watch me make things like tortoises from egg boxes. I put happy faces on them because happy faces make me smile.

Gail Collier I like going in the little bumper cars at the fair. I crash into other people and we all laugh. Most of all I like to chase Mummy and Daddy and Granddad because they think it's funny.

Alexander McDowall I am happy when I go to the zoo because the noises make me laugh. I would not mind whoever I went with. I would like it if it was sunny.

Marcella Edwards Christmas makes me happy because when we get presents you get so excited and at night Father Christmas comes.

Arabella Wallace Happiness is waterskiing. I love whizzing through the waves. Stalking makes me happy. I love to hear the wind whispering in the ferns and seeing the lordly antlers of the stag. I love to wake up in the morning and to swim; it makes me happy. Riding makes me happy but I don't like riding a donkey. I love riding in the woods in the morning. The smell of the dew, the sun, makes me happy. Running my hand through corn makes me happy.

Emma Ludford Happiness is riding and swimming. The smell of burning pine makes me happy. I love riding my bike and playing netball. I like reading and drawing.

Olivia Robinson Playing my violin, the piano and the recorder. I like making music. Happiness comes in sports like playing tennis and ball games like sevens. I like going on holiday to cosy cottages in Wales and seeing the lovely view there is in Scotland and hearing the sound of the sea in the Isle of Wight and seeing Blackgang Chine in the Isle of Wight. That is what makes me happy!

Catherine Hatt-Cook The sun – Daddy showing me photographs – friends coming to stay – stones with pictures – pretty pictures and shells – going to Cornwall on holiday.

Naomi Bache I like to go to parties and give my friends nice presents. I like winning games and I love party cakes. I like looking pretty in my best dress.

Toby Thorogood Singing. Country walks with family dog. Building sandcastles. Picnic lunches. Playing on go-kart and bicycle and climbing trees. Having friends to play. Bedtime stories. Colouring. School. Tea beside a big log fire in the winter. Bathtime. Fun fairs and sweets.

George Howe

The Sheriff of Nottingham is alive and well. George Howe has an office that is over a thousand years old and he has found that Robin Hood folklore is quite a selling point in attracting tourists to Nottingham, and has posed for a thousand photographs, assuming the most menacing and glowering appearance which is expected of a Sheriff of Nottingham.

Before he was elected, George was general manager of the largest food store in Nottingham. After his year in office, George, who is sixty-five, will retire.

Ever since a memorial statue was built to honour Robin Hood, vandals have been removing arrows from his quiver. To foil these present-day outlaws, George has redesigned the statue with riveted fibreglass arrows.

When I visit schools as the holder of the office of the famous Sheriff of Nottingham, the school children's little faces light up and they are all agog with excitement and wonder, anxious to ask questions about the office of sheriff.

Hospital visiting also gives me happiness and humility; to see patients beaming when I visit them to chat about their illnesses or, in some cases, their disabilities. When I shake hands in greeting to them, they all grip hands firmly to show their thanks. Most important of all, happiness must be genuine and sincere in every instance.

Peter Ingram

Peter Ingram is a coachbuilder and painter who is keeping alive the gypsy ways by making and storing the old horse-drawn wagons. Some he sells to gorjos, *non-gypsies, and it is easy to see their appeal with the romantic image they conjure up.*

Peter is a true gypsy. But he is no longer 'nomadic' – he lives with his artist wife in a picturesque Hampshire village. He speaks fluent Romany and believes in most of the gypsy ways. He is opposed to compulsory education and more than a touch superstitious.

Peter has started a gypsy museum. He believes anyone who is a romantic is a gypsy at heart.

Moaning – I'm a great moaner – but it makes me happy!

Knowing that I can harness up my horse and van and take to the road if need be, light a fire and cook a meal in the rain, catch a rabbit, make a rod and blanket tent, make clothes pegs, baskets and wooden flowers and earn a living day by day makes me happy.

Having a large wad of notes in my pocket makes me happy. At the moment the thing that makes me most happy is driving my horse Sam and the flat-cart. Sam is a skewbald, a real gypsy horse – and holding up the traffic makes me even happier.

Spring makes me happy; the fresh green leaves on the hawthorn hedges; the first primrose on a mossy bank and the cuckoo. The cuckoo, because as soon as I hear it, I think of Ambrose Smith talking to George Borrow (nineteenth century). The conversation went something like this:

AMBROSE SMITH: 'The cuckoo and the gypsy are very similar, brother.'
GEORGE BORROW: 'Why so, brother?'
AMBROSE SMITH: 'The cuckoo comes in the spring, has no place of his own, lays the eggs where it can and everyone chaffs him. But if he didn't turn up in the spring everyone would miss him.'
GEORGE BORROW: 'Quite so, brother, and the same with the gypsy, brother.'
AMBROSE SMITH: 'Aye, brother.'

And so to see horse and van on the road or an encampment with a van and tents, a whisp of woodsmoke drifting up from the stickfire, a van in the firelight, a plume of smoke coming from the chimney of my van on a cold winter's day – all fill my eyes with tears of happiness.

Hearing my canary sing makes me happy. Hearing my Alsatian bark at the trippers who infest my village makes me happy.

Working for myself makes me happy, perhaps not the start of it, the hard bit, but the finished job – all gold leaf and fine lines and scholled – like a big Christmas cake – I walk away and look at the van – restored to its former glory.

Meeting a good old-fashioned tramp and giving him a quid makes me happy, although there aren't so many now.

Listening to Jimmy Rodgers and Hank Williams (old Country and Western records) makes me happy.

Two glasses of my wife's home-made elderberry wine makes me happiest of all!

Jackie Jaguer

On the battlefield of Hastings in 1066, King Harold was positively identified by the word Edith, his wife's name, tattooed above his heart.

The tattoo is a varyingly fashionable adornment, never more in vogue than when King Edward VII had one (a discreet butterfly on the shoulder), and set the style for Edwardians. Churchill's mother had one.

Jackie Jaguer has been a tattooist for four years. She was taught by her husband. It's laborious but artistic work. The customer picks a design from 300 patterns ranging from a popular 'MUM' or a heart to something intimate (or obscene). They vary in price from three pounds to over a hundred.

Jackie uses an electric high-speed drill with eight needles that puncture the skin and applies an indelible vegetable dye. There's always profuse bleeding which has to be wiped away every few seconds, in fact when Jackie first saw a tattoo being done, she fainted.

One thing that really comes to mind was when my dog had puppies . . . six appealing little faces, with Sheba, their mother, looking as proud as punch, watching them grow up and develop their various little characters.

Of course I could go on indefinitely, travelling, kissing, caressing. Almost anything makes me happy. A good meal, nice clothes, a rave-up, a joke, beautiful things to look at, a child's face on receiving a gift, lots of money, like a good win at the casino. The satisfaction of putting an extra good tattoo on someone makes me happy.

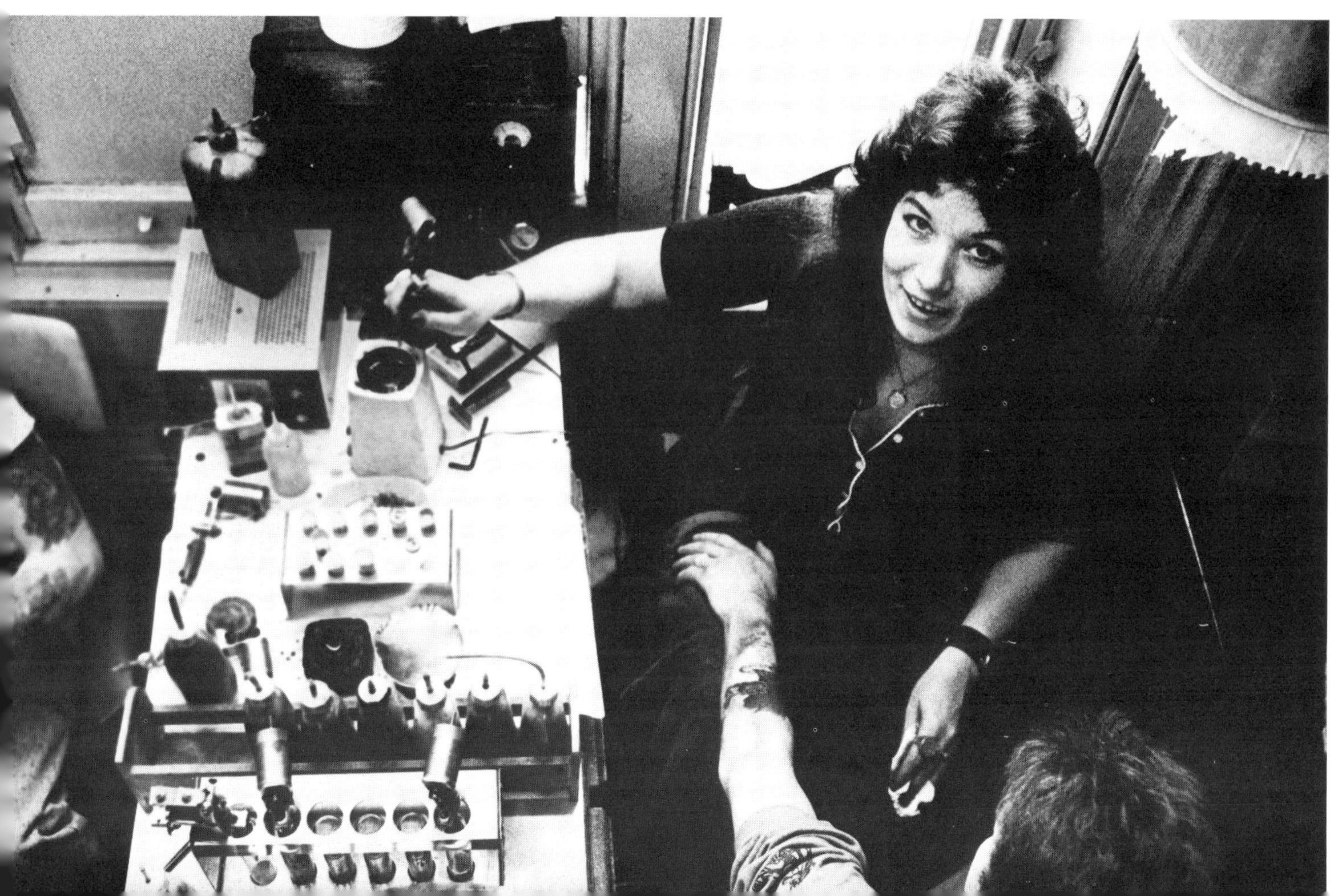

Dr Immanuel Jakobovits

As Chief Rabbi, Dr Immanuel Jakobovits is secular leader of nearly half a million Jews in this country.

Dr Jakobovits emigrated to England as a refugee from Nazi Germany while still a teenager and entered the ministry at the age of twenty. Before his thirtieth birthday he was called to Dublin as Chief Rabbi of Ireland, where he remained for ten years. After a spell in America and Israel he was installed as Chief Rabbi of the British Commonwealth in 1967.

What makes me happy is the success of my children in perpetuating my life. It is contentment at work, the excitement of challenge, and the cultivation of friendships.

To bring a smile to a careworn face, solace and companionship to a lost soul, a sense of purpose to a perplexed mind, and the balm of faith to the wounds of despair – these, too, are ingredients of happiness.

My happiness also has more mundane features. A caravan holiday in the inspiring solitude of nature's majesty, a book on exploring the mysteries of faith or space, a group of students quizzing me on my specialized interest in medical ethics, or lighting the pipe to inhale inspiration for the next move in a chess game can occasionally contribute to the enjoyment of life.

However, I believe that happiness – like honour, according to the ancient Jewish sages – escapes those who pursue it, and overtakes those who flee from it. In any event, man is born to make the times good, rather than to have a good time.

Derek Jameson

Derek Jameson, a cockney from the Hackney Marshes, an illegitimate child who never knew his father, is now editor of the Daily Express *and editor-in-chief of the* Daily Star.

Derek's initial ambition was to become a novelist and learn the mechanics of a literary career through journalism. But with successive promotions in the newspaper world, the more uncertain work of a novelist soon appeared less exciting.

Derek's first job at fourteen was as a messenger boy for Reuters. He was made to rewrite the first story he ever covered sixteen times. Before becoming a national daily editor he was a reporter, features writer, sub-editor, picture editor, night editor and Northern editor.

Oh God, to be happy. There is not a lot of it about. In this crazy age, the thing is to keep ahead of the game. Work, struggle, succeed. Save the laughter for fools.

There is no bigger fool than Tommy Cooper. Just see him standing there, that immense bulk, totally insulated in his own magic world of madness. He is the one who got away. No wonder we laugh. I do not know if *he* is happy, but he makes *me* happy. And millions of other people.

Koko

If you consider it an ordeal to pose for one snapshot in the garden, or an imposition to wait around while your spouse attempts to focus on both the sweeping Costa del Sol and your sunburnt face, then spare a thought for the model. It may take a day for a photographer to get the effect he's looking for – and he generally asks for facial and physical contortions that only an Argentinian strongman would require.

In a typical working week, Koko modelled a bikini on Brighton Pier, where the weather was so cold she was asked not to breathe out (and show her breath steaming); she modelled a full-length sable coat with high heels at three fashion shows in one day, and sat in a bubble-bath for eight hours to advertise a waterproof eye-liner.

Fortunately Koko enjoys the constant grooming and physical attention a model must lavish on herself, and is well trained in the arts of beauty care. In Calabar, Nigeria, where she was brought up, she was a buyer for a cosmetics firm, and when she moved to London three years ago she took a beauty therapy course while training as a hairdresser.

According to Koko, the success of a model depends on her ability to act a role. It's not enough to smile at a camera. If you wear a plunging neckline you must look sexy; if you're sporting diamonds and furs, you must look haughty and inaccessible.

And it doesn't hurt, if like Koko you are almost six foot with a 35-24-36 figure.

There's almost nothing in the world that makes me happier than dancing. Physically, it's one of the most exciting sensations I know; and mentally, well, it's complete satisfaction.

There's something about the feeling I get on a dance floor which is more fulfilling than almost anything else. I suppose it's because dancing is such a complete experience. The rhythm of the music seems to take me over and touch my soul. The physical aftermath leaves me with boundless energy and a zest for life – without which my existence would have little meaning.

Angela Lambert

With only four months to go before the birth of her first baby, Angela Lambert is planning to stop work as a secretary.

Ever since Angela left her home town of Maidstone in Kent to live in London, she has worked as a temporary secretary. It's a fabulous opportunity to see how businesses are run, and Angela has worked in many varied professions. Unfortunately, a temp is often left the most unpleasant tasks, typing form letters, filing, or making endless cups of tea.

After work Angela returns home to look after husband Robert whose greatest culinary achievement was to poach one egg six years ago. Nor is housework Robert's forte as he would have trouble distinguishing a dust rag from a pillowcase, Angela says. But like countless working women, Angela manages to cope with the added labour of the most arduous job – that of housewife.

Waking up at three a.m. and realizing there are another five hours until I have to get up gives me a moment of intense happiness. Or, when I am so mad because I've spilt all the coffee I have just ground on the floor and Robert walks through the door and makes me laugh and feel good.

But the thing that makes me happiest of all is the thought of this little creature kicking around inside me reminding me constantly that it is not so long until Bumble (er, that's its name) arrives, and all the joy and happiness to come.

Dennis Lane

Apart from a few years during the war, Dennis Lane has been pulling pints for the last six decades. He was even born in a pub, the one his parents ran in Essex. Dennis now owns the Sussex Arms in Tunbridge Wells, a pub that dates back to 1630. The Arms offers a huge selection of beer – more than 37 varieties of English beers, and about 40 different lagers from around the world.

The border between Sussex and Kent runs through the pub, and depending which room you choose, you can decide in which county you prefer to drink.

The specialities of the house are Dennis's Hangover Remedy (a large Guinness with a healthy booster of port), and his Chilli Burton (a strong ale with chillis and herbs), which is reputed to keep out the cold throughout the winter.

It's been said that the Brit is partial to a drop of beer now and then, and with 74,484 pubs and 80,000 clubs and off-licences in the country there is no difficulty in his finding a place to drink it.

Happiness is that ecstatic feeling communicated between beings when they are giving out and receiving on the same wavelength. Contentment may be achieved by oneself, but happiness always needs more than one, and is only two bottles of champagne away.

Commander Roger Lane-Nott

When Commander Roger Lane-Nott leaves home, he doesn't keep in touch. No cards, no letters, not even a telephone call. He commands HMS Splendid, *one of Britain's nuclear submarines, and no one on board is allowed to break radio silence for the entire seventy days at (well, under) sea.*

Britain now has sixteen nuclear submarines, and they are truly devastating fighting machines. With nuclear propulsion, a submarine can stay indefinitely under water and has a world-wide radius of action and a bristling armoury of missiles, harpoons and torpedoes with a range of up to three thousand miles. Another awesome feature is the price – £150 million.

There are 115 men on board the Splendid, *and Roger is the only man with his own cabin. He admits that lack of privacy is the least enjoyable feature of the submariner's lot.*

Roger is undeterred by the rigorous life. At thirty-four he is in a position of great responsibility and loves commanding his own submarine. After forty, when a man is considered too old to captain a submarine, Roger's ambition is to become librarian of BBC's Grandstand Videotape collection!

Happiness is 500 feet in a force-ten gale.

Happiness for me is like a double-headed coin, for I enjoy being at sea beneath the waves and I enjoy being at home with my family. I joined the Royal Navy for reasons which today are unfashionable. Loyalty and service to Queen and country and the prospect of a challenging, demanding and varied career.

Separation from my family is never good, but the return from sea is. You have so much to catch up on and returning from cramped conditions sharpens your appreciation of home. I think I have had about 150 second honeymoons in my submarine career – so far! It is a case of 'absence makes the heart grow fonder' rather than 'out of sight, out of mind' for my wife and I.

SIGN OF THE ANGEL

John Levis

There's a village in Wiltshire where time seems to have stood still. Half-timbered houses covered with roses, cobblestone roads, tiny corner-shops and lush green fields abound.

To stop the twentieth century from intruding and destroying the medieval pastoral community of Lacock, the National Trust has stepped in and bought the village, lock, stock and barrel.

John Levis runs the Sign of the Angel, a fourteenth-century inn, with his wife, son and daughter-in-law. With antique beds, roaring fires and candle-light, plus impeccable food, John's inn is in keeping with the beauty and uniqueness of this extraordinary village.

It's halfway between cheerfulness and ecstasy. I can contrive cheerfulness, but ecstasy is God-given. Cheerfulness is the secret stock on which I can graft happiness.

Happiness you only know about and miss when you haven't got it.

I can feel happiness most often when I have satisfied my customers. When I listen to someone unwinding when they have come to stay with me, they make me realize how lucky I am, which I need because being an innkeeper can become like all jobs.

I only have to look out of my back door to know I'm happy. I'm simple and get simpler, thank God. I can see beauty in trees and bushes, fields and wet grass. I think keeping cows and hens, as I do, makes you see the importance of sun, rain, mist and all the other things that go to make up a day.

Happiness is a gift. You can easily give thanks when you have it. One of its great ingredients is contentment with your lot, not to envy or covet.

Stan Lomax

At Claridge's there are two staff for every guest. When William Claridge bought the hotel to which he gave his name in 1838, he intended the luxury and first-class standard of service which he started to last for ever.

He never knew Stan Lomax but one senses he would have approved. Stan has been head doorman at Claridge's for ten years. His grandeur and dignity set the tone for the opulence inside.

Heads of state, film stars, foreign kings and queens, millionaires – Stan has met them all. But he only doffs his hat for 'my' royalty. There are in-built rewards and problems in the occupation Stan has chosen. Four times hooligans have made off with his top hat (a powerful sprinter, Stan has recovered it twice); he has shut a taxi door on a customer's leg, and once on a lady's skirt. On the plus side, Stan enjoys meeting people, being in the fresh air, and watching the constant stream of pretty girls who walk by.

Firstly it must be my family, I've been married twenty-eight years and have two married daughters, the eldest having two sons, and to know that I am DAD makes me happy, very happy.

At work, I am a doorman at Claridge's Hotel. The job has its ups and downs like any other, but most of the time I am very happy. I've got to know a great number of people, from all over the world, important people, heads of state and royalty, and I welcome them to the hotel. To shake hands and wish each other well can only make me feel happy (it helps with the wages too).

In my spare time, I like to play darts, and I am fortunate to be a little better than the average player. I have quite a number of trophies I have won over past years, but to play well is the thing that makes me happy. Yes, I'm happy to keep adding to my trophy shelf, because to win is a happy feeling, and then you soon forget the games you lose.

One other thing that makes me feel happy is the freedom of the countryside. I live in a council tower-block, in my opinion a concrete prison, and to get away from the noise of the traffic and buildings, to take my dog for a long walk where there are trees and grass, makes me happy. I must be getting old because I love it, and to be able to live in the country permanently would make me feel very happy.

Lord Longford

Francis Augnier Pakenham, Seventh Earl of Longford, is a jack-of-all-trades. Former Leader of the House of Lords, First Lord of the Admiralty, Lord in Waiting to King George VI, Under-Secretary of State for the War Office, Lord Privy Seal – he's been them all, which makes his curriculum vitae sound like a Gilbert and Sullivan opera.

He converted from the Protestant faith at the age of thirty-five and is now a devout Catholic, and his life has been coloured by his devotion. In his campaign for penal reform he has earned plenty of public abuse, especially with his championing of the moors murderess, Myra Hindley. But she's just one of the hundreds of prisoners he is helping.

Lord Longford is also a publisher and author. He is currently working on a biography of Richard Nixon.

Happiness is not the highest value in life, that can only be virtue. But happiness is surely a good second with beauty treading hard on its heels. Is Socrates dissatisfied better than a pig satisfied? Personally I think so.

I am made most happy by being loved, and happiest of all by being loved by someone who loves me, as I love her.

Of course a religious answer could be given to this question, but I am writing in human terms.

Next comes gratitude. I am made enormously happy if people are grateful to me. Frequently I do not deserve it, but whether I deserve it or not, gratitude far more than repays any exertion I could have possibly made on anyone's behalf.

Joe Loss

To the sound of Joe Loss and his Big Band, a half-century of dance crazes has been tried out – from the Charleston to the Cha-Cha, the Quickstep, Rumba, Foxtrot and Tango.

Joe's first musical job was playing the violin at the Coliseum theatre in Spitalfield where he was born. He played accompaniment to the silent films – behind a thick velvet curtain. When the talkies started, Joe couldn't wait to get out in front of a live audience.

At seventy-one, Joe doesn't let up. He records three albums a year, tours around the country and last year played right round the world, including a concert in China.

Joe is a great favourite of the Royal Family and has often played at Buckingham Palace and Windsor Castle. Whether it's the Palace, or a roadside café, Joe never tires of playing his music.

Happiness is my business. Over my fifty years as a bandleader I've played for millions of dancers and I can't say that I've ever seen any one of them looking miserable.

But away from my professional life, I'm happy sharing my life with my wife of forty years, Mildred, and my two children. Now, thanks to my daughter Jennifer, I have three grandchildren also, and I'm never happier than when I'm with them at the weekends. Of course, Jennifer always chides me for spoiling them, but isn't that what grandparents are for? I love to see young people happy. And despite what we read about the frailties of the young, I think they're much maligned.

Being British makes me happy, despite all the knockers. I returned from my fifth world cruise on the *QE2* in April and although I've played many times on this magnificent ship, I never cease to wonder at the craftsmanship that causes thousands of people to come and look at it wherever we dock throughout the world.

Happiness means peace of mind and whatever our station of life, you can't buy happiness. It's contentment, a feeling of well-being, the joy of family life, the thrill of an achievement, a kind word, a helpful deed and the ability to laugh at all things so long as it isn't at the expense of someone else.

Michael McCrum

Six hundred years and several score headmasters on, Eton College is still thriving. Parents who want their children to tread the stamping ground of twenty prime ministers, countless dukes, marquesses, earls, and even the occasional lowly Honourable, must put down their offspring's name at birth. And there's a one-in-four chance of his getting in.

Michael McCrum has just retired after ten years as headmaster. He was a don at Cambridge and headmaster of Tonbridge before that. With 1,250 boys under his care, he may chat with a boy on his first day at school, perhaps discuss a problem, and then not see him again for four or five years. (Each boy, however, has a house master and tutor, who know him well.)

Public floggings and fagging are no longer fashionable at Eton, although in severe circumstances a headmaster will send a boy home for a period (rustication) and inevitably, boys being boys, must reluctantly use his cane on one or two recalcitrant trouser seats.

If you're thinking of putting down your young Algernon or Louise (it's rumoured Eton will be coeducational by the end of the decade), the fees are £1,000 a term.

Happiness for me is a deep inner serenity of spirit, that feels with Mother Julian of Norwich 'All shall be well, and all shall be well, and all manner of thing shall be well.' As one knows that the sun is there even when it is obscured by clouds, so true happiness is a permanent state of mind, unruffled by temporary misfortunes or setbacks, based on the knowledge that 'underneath are the everlasting arms'. Behind the transient phenomena of our daily lives there is a permanent One. The Greeks searched for this unity in diversity and nearly discovered it. The answer came from Palestine, and the One proved to be triune, because happiness is an active not passive state of mind. At the heart of the universe, at the centre of our being, the peace and joy associated with happiness spring from faith in the triune One which is bound up with faith in the essential 'belovedness' and 'lovingness' of other people.

Charles McFadyen

It may surprise you to know there is one household object that is still hand-produced.

At the Armitage Shanks factory in Glasgow, Charlie McFadyen hand-finishes thirty WCs a day. He lovingly moulds and smooths out the clay until the throne is perfectly formed – and then he sees it no more as mechanical processes take over.

The toilet is taken on a mechanical odyssey. It is chairlifted to a kiln and fired for days, fitted with all household and plumbing accoutrements and then sprayed in white, turquoise, pink, sienna or caspian blue.

Charlie is a mad football fan and runs an amateur team in Paisley. Naturally, Charlie gets teased about his job – but too many cracks and a joker might be warming the bench for a whole season.

Happiness to me is my wife and family, I have three boys of 17, 20 and 23 and two girls, 12 and 15. The youngest is cerebrally retarded. She can't talk and is still on nappies – but to me she is everything that happiness can bring. She has a smile that lights up her whole face and when she laughs everyone in the house has to laugh whether you are down in the dumps or not. She keeps everyone on their toes with the antics she gets up to. The place just wouldn't be the same without her. She can turn a dreary day into something special and seeing her improving day by day is something that only parents with handicapped children can appreciate.

The sister and nurses at Elderslee Hospital where she goes daily are doing a great job. No amount of money could be great enough for all the dedication that the staff put into their work. I know that it will take a long while for Alison ever to be perfect, but just to see the happiness that she brings to our family is something that has to be seen to be believed.

Sue MacGregor

Woman's Hour, *one of the longest-running programmes in radio history, was first broadcast in October 1946, and was presented by a man for three months. It has been presented by a woman ever since.*

Sue MacGregor has fronted the programme for the past eight years, and it is estimated that over a million women tune in at two minutes past two every weekday afternoon to listen to her.

Woman's Hour *comes from a windowless studio so far underneath Broadcasting House that one can hear the rumble of the Circle and Metropolitan lines. There are two studio managers and a producer who put out the programme live, although some of the items have been taped before. The interview, letters, serials, etc, are carefully timed; each second of the fifty-eight-minute programme must be accounted for as the three o'clock news must go out on time.*

Sue seems unflappable. No traces of nerves. She worked on World at One *before* Woman's Hour *and in South Africa, where she was brought up, edited and presented a radio programme at the age of twenty.*

It's in simple things: in enjoying being with young children, and their delicate innocence; in walking on a mountainside in hot sunshine; in feeling that possibly you're falling in love; in hearing a special piece of music unexpectedly; in being with friends and, sometimes, in being alone. Certainly happiness has nothing much to do with money and possessions, and almost everything to do with people. But a lifetime of happiness? I'm inclined to agree with Shaw. No man alive could bear it: it would be hell on earth.

Norris McWhirter

'The authors who have written the highest selling title are Norris Dewar McWhirter and his late twin brother Alan Ross McWhirter, editors and compilers of the Guinness Book of Records *first published in 1955. Global sales in 19 languages by May 1980 reached over 45,000,000 copies'* – Guinness Book of Records.

The idea for the book originated with Sir Hugh Beaver, the managing director of Guinness in the early 1950s. He had been out shooting one day in Ireland by the river Slaney when a golden plover flew above him at high speed and he missed it. In the pub, the conversation turned controversial as he argued whether the golden plover was the fastest game bird in Europe. Recourse to various encyclopedias in the library failed to settle the argument and Sir Hugh realized that records were just the things that started pub arguments all over the country and it was time somebody produced a book of records to settle this kind of dispute.

Norris and his brother were running a fact and figures agency for newspapers and seemed to be experts on all manner of records. They were summoned to meet the Guinness board who were so impressed that a decision was immediately taken to set up a publishing subsidiary.

A visitor from another planet, if he were to get hold of the book, would think we were an extraordinary race. The hope of a mention in the book seems to inspire people to unbelievable acts of lunacy. Norris has personally witnessed many of the records.

Each year the gauntlet is thrown down – more eels are swallowed per minute, more hula-hoops gyrated simultaneously, the longest moustache grows another inch, the tallest tree another foot; which means that a quarter of the book must be revised each edition.

Unlike blood pressure or a bank balance, there remains no actual measurement or unit of happiness. Since the concept of this book is imaginative and original, then perhaps you might permit me to invent such a unit. The obvious unit is the decibliss, such that on a scale of zero to ten, the ultimate 10 equals the state of absolute bliss. I think very few of us have experienced in ourselves or in others sustained values in excess of the heavenly 7.

The decibliss scale, however, is not merely a positive 0 to 10. It can also be negative down to the utter hopelessness and dejectedness of the suicidal level at minus 9.

Happiness is, however, usually thought of introspectively. Given the fundaments of reasonable health, prosperity and freedom, how is it that some people can rise above the mere median zero of being neither happy nor unhappy? The art seems to depend upon the wisdom of the individuals' sense of values and their personal philosophy embracing that elusive balance of moderation between selfishness and selflessness. In this, nothing seems so productive as that tranquil and secure upbringing by parents which modern industrialized society with its ever-earning mothers and its television *kultur* makes increasingly rare.

The pursuit of happiness is an activity, often demanding and almost invariably frustrating, which is simply not exhibited in a naturally happy person. Those who possess have no need to pursue. Pursuit excludes that massive calm and quiet confidence of the happily married monogamist who has the helm in his own hand and who is inner-directed. The headlong hedonist or the miserable millionaire do not excite universal envy.

Two sayings have always impressed themselves on my receptive Scottish upbringing. One is that 'Perfection is finality and finality is death' – wrongly and recently attributed to James Stephens. The other is by Duc de la Rochefoucauld in the seventeenth century: 'Man can only achieve true satisfaction by self-denial.' Maybe he was reflecting upon that ultimate and in the end inevitably disastrous extravagance – the building of the Palace of Versailles.

However, all this seems like a rather long introduction to a short postscript because I believe I am intended to reveal to you what makes me happy rather than to philosophize about happiness in general.

The best way to do that is to recall the happiest

moments of a life still a decade and a half short of nature's 'allotted span'. I am grateful for being asked to undertake an exercise upon which one would not otherwise dream of embarking. Recalling happinesses allows them to be relived. It underlines also how people change over the years.

My earliest happy memories are of being allowed to stay up late, of being read to with my twin by the fire by my mother; of bananas and a chocolate log-cake which were always in short supply and of Wednesdays when our sport-starved kindergarten school had netball games. Later at preparatory school, bliss was hot buttered toast under a silver cover in a Pullman from London to Eastbourne when returning for a mid-term dental appointment, having knocked out two front teeth on a roller-skating rink.

On reflection, I cannot really recall that my twin and I had any really unhappy experiences during that seemingly endless process known as education that goes on formally for fifteen years and informally for ever. The absence of trauma and hence of contrast possibly muted the experiences of intense happiness, though I recollect our naturally competitive streak, verging on the combative, gave intense pleasure in the heat of sporting competition.

Wartime austerity and rationing lent magic to crumpets and to powdered cream. Such magic would have been otherwise unknown to affluent children in time of peace. Wartime separation from my twin during naval service lent a magic to a reunion which otherwise would never have been experienced. An unforgettable moment was when my immediate family circle re-formed without any casualties round the drawing-room fire in November 1946, in a house in a road which had received thirty-four bombs during the war years. With the world and life stretching ahead, that was perhaps the most memorable moment of happiness until marriage and two children took over with vicarious happinesses.

Eric Malpass

Eric Malpass is a gentle and very persevering man. This, he says, is fortunate, for he has had to wait a long time for his present enormous literary success. Born in 1910, he was forced to give up hopes of a university education on the death of his father, and went instead to work in a bank. It was not until after the Second World War, on his return to the bank, that he seriously began to write in his spare time. Since then he has written innumerable short stories, winning the Observer *short story competition in 1954, and four novels. His first book,* Beefy Jones, *published in 1956, was awarded the Palma d'Oro in Italy for the best humorous novel of the year. Even so, it was not until the publication of* Morning's at Seven, *eight years later, that he was able to consider leaving the bank and devoting all his time to writing.* Morning's at Seven, *a bestseller in Germany, has now been published in America and in every European country except Norway. It has also been filmed.*

Malpass and his wife live quietly near Nottingham, in an area he has known and loved all his life. They have one son, and two grandchildren. His next book, Oh, My Darling Daughter, *is to be published next year. In spite of his novels' warmth and their light-hearted surface, he is a man deeply concerned by the threat of violence always present in contemporary society, and – as is clear from* Morning's at Seven *– his writing reflects this concern.*

Although his success has enabled him to resign from the bank, it has brought with it many other commitments, so that in fact his writing life is little changed. About the only difference, he says, is that he can now read all *of the* Daily Telegraph, *instead of only the front page.*

I do not agree with the American Declaration of Independence.

Not because I either wish or expect the United States to revert to colonial status; but because I think the resounding phrase with which it ends is false. Life, yes. Liberty, certainly. But 'the pursuit of happiness'? This surely is a chimera. Is not man pursuing happiness like a child chasing a rainbow in a summer meadow? Or like Alice who found the Red Queen getting further away the faster she walked towards her?

No. Happiness cannot be pursued. But it can, and must, be bought. And the price is very high.

It must be bought with unhappiness, and suffering, and knowledge of self, and knowledge of good and evil. Only those who have endured war can enjoy the happiness of peace. Only those who have known pain can know the happiness of body's ease. Only those who have known the struggle can know the full joy of the mountain peak.

But another form of happiness has no price, demands no payment. There are in a man's life occasional, and very rare, moments when for no reason whatever he will know a sudden lightening of the spirit, a lifting of the heart so that he says, in wonder and delight, 'I am happy.' He may be walking to post a letter, digging up potatoes, standing at his window to watch the fall of the snow. He may be with chosen friends, in his garden, on a summer's evening. And suddenly this gossamer thing will touch him, this evanescent thing of quiet joy. It will touch him; and it will pass, in moments, like April sunlight across the mountains. Yet, looking back over the years, he will always remember that moment, and will say, 'Then, I was happy, unaccountably happy. For no reason whatever.' And he will ask himself whether perhaps an angel passed by.

Yehudi Menuhin

Although he has been playing his violin for six decades and has been unanimously declared one of the world's finest musicians, Yehudi Menuhin still works on his scales and exercises every day of his life.

Many great violinists start as prodigies, but even among those Yehudi Menuhin was exceptional. He heard his first concert when he was two. Before he was four he asked for a violin, and for lessons when he was five. At seven he gave his first concert performance. Yehudi Menuhin was brought up in San Francisco where his Russian-born father taught Hebrew at the university. He never went to school but was educated at home and trained in music by no less than the conductor of the San Francisco Symphony Orchestra.

He does much work for charity. His attitude towards the world seems to be one of courteous concern coupled with unbounded gallantry. Of all the causes to which he is committed there are three which are closest to his heart. One is Amnesty International. Another is the Puffin Club which two hundred thousand children formed to collect money to buy an island off the Scottish coast for puffins to live in safety. And then there is the school he founded at Stoke d'Abernon in Surrey whose pupils from the age of six are taught to play a variety of instruments.

Yehudi Menuhin now lives in London. He is married with four children. He once went to a Rolling Stones concert. He did not enjoy it. The three Bs – Bach, Beethoven and Brahms – continue to be his favourite composers.

What I call happiness is a dynamic equilibrium, in the first place between oneself and one's conscience, that is an inner equilibrium; secondly, between oneself and one's life partner and family; thirdly, between oneself and one's community, race, nation, religion; fourthly, between oneself and nature; and finally, between oneself and God, the latter an equilibrium rather more static than dynamic, which we call bliss – perhaps a state associated with death.

Happiness and the pursuit of happiness is a noble human prospect, nowhere more tangible than in beautiful work, well done – and particularly in music, itself an abstraction and sublimation of all factors, complexities and conflicts.

Keith Miller

When Keith Miller at seventeen left Jamaica with his parents, the only image he had of this country was from old films. He had seen the cold, fog-shrouded streets of London in countless black-and-white mystery films, and heard the echoing footsteps in dark alleys while flickering gas lamps hissed ominously. London seemed light-years away from the happy-go-lucky tropical island that was his home.

But life here wasn't as Keith had feared. He trained as a mechanic, starting as an apprentice with a salary of £5 a week and qualifying after the standard five years of training.

Keith has been living here for more than twenty years, sharing a house with his brother in Balham, just south of the Thames. He now works at a car stereo shop, installing radios, tape machines and the occasional (it's a very upmarket car stereo shop) telephone and television set.

What really makes you happy? Incredible, isn't it? The one thing we all want and long for and yet when asked the question we start stuttering and fail to give a reasonable answer. I can think of a hundred things that would make me happy for a little while but in the end the novelty wears off. I have never considered myself a happy person. Happy-go-lucky, yes. But happy completely, no. I've always had a certain amount of discontent about myself, because I do not think I've achieved anything in life so far – I mean going back as far as my schooldays in Jamaica. I

was one of a group of kids picked from our class and told we were to be given extra lessons in preparation for our GCE examinations. We all felt superior to the other kids. As it turned out I was kicked out of the class because I didn't do my homework and the teacher got fed up with my excuses. The real reason was that I preferred spending the evenings after classes at a racing stable, talking horses with apprentice jockey friends of mine. I have since met two of the guys from that GCE class, one's an assistant manager in a bank, and the other's a senior Customs officer. I wasn't very happy with myself. I've played soccer for a club for almost a full season, only to get fed up and leave, and then hear from someone that the team went on to win a cup or a medal. Again I lost out.

I love parties and being in with a group of fun-loving people. I am always ready for action, if it means having a good time with people I like to be with. I get a satisfied sort of feeling if I think I've made people happy, and that in turn affects me in the same way. Dull people are just not on with me. I get a lot of fun out of taking the mickey out of my friends. They don't seem to mind. We all laugh at one another's past experiences, and at times even one's private life has been known to cause a few chuckles. I am at my happiest when I'm with my close friends having fun. To me being happy also means being contented – I think I'd be contented if I was doing the sort of job I enjoyed and was being well paid for doing it. When people are contented, happiness is just around the corner. So in the long run I think that's what should make me happy. The rest follows.

Patrick Moore

Because of an illness as a youngster, Patrick Moore never went to school. He was educated privately. At the age of six he found, read and mastered two books. One was about the solar system, the other about gravitational forces. It took a few years more to save £7 10/- to buy a telescope, but by then his commitment was unquestionable.

The Sky at Night, *Patrick's own television programme, has been broadcast now since 1957 which makes it the longest running continuous programme in the world (barring the news) and has made star-gazing a hobby for millions.*

Patrick is a whirlwind of energy. He finds time for dozens of activities. He is secretary of his home cricket club (Selsey in Sussex), a composer of xylophone music and author of more than sixty books (which he types on his 1908 Woodstock typewriter).

He has been awarded an honorary doctorate from Lancaster University, a citation from the Royal Astronomical Society, and consistently over the years from a fashion magazine the title of 'Unbestdressed man on TV'.

In talking about 'happiness', I think one must distinguish between selfish motives and less selfish ones! All of us have our own ambitions. I know I have. For instance, I would like to go to the Moon; alas, no chance – at the age of fifty-seven I am too ancient even if I could muster the other qualifications. I would like to make a century in a cricket match; again, no chance – I bat like the leg-spin bowler I am. And I would like to compose a waltz as good as those of Strauss, but I know my limitations.

What would make me really happy would be to see a world which fulfils its potential. After all, we live on what could be a pleasant planet. There is plenty of food (and energy) to go round if only we could organize ourselves. We could do it – if we come to our senses in time. There is no reason why not, apart from defects in the basic character of *Homo sapiens*. And if I could be certain of this, and if (a most unlikely event!) I could play even a microscopic part in bringing it about, then I would know real happiness.

Sir Jeremy Morse

Do you have a cosy, intimate relationship with your bank manager, dropping in every now and then to pass the time of day, exchanging the odd joke? Or do you fear those inevitable encounters with a man you generally meet under less than amicable conditions? Sir Jeremy Morse is chairman of Lloyds Bank and head of 2,375 branches in Britain alone. Although Lloyds is the smallest of the four big banks, more than six million people have accounts at Lloyds. And yet Sir Jeremy is a most approachable man, friendly, polite and not the slightest bit intimidating.

Weather makes me happy and children's parties. I love seeing old truths confirmed, and finding that some great governing idea from the past or some famous line of poetry still fits and helps to explain the world. The continuity of great minds, and the continuity of family life, which are our roots, both make me happy.

In another broader sense of the word, I could say that I have so far had a happy life. But, as the Greeks wisely said, call no man happy until he is dead.

Jack Morton

Jack Morton is retiring next year after a half-century of working in coal mines. We met him 600 feet below the fertile Northumberland terrain, at the Blenkinsopp Colliery, where he was supervising the blasting of a new tunnel.

There have been a lot of changes in the business since Jack started as a boy – for one thing, horses used to draw out the coal loads. 'But when they took out the ponies they left in the asses,' says Jack.

It has been said that without happiness drudgery has no compensation. It would be an insult to all miners to compare their highly skilled craft with drudgery. Physically it is a heavy and dangerous job, but by virtue of its danger, it breeds a courage, a sense of humour and a comradeship which is unique and rarely found in any other profession.

To work among miners and with them and to have contributed to the success of a thriving place, this for me is happiness.

Lance-Corporal Joss Murray

Lance-Corporal Joss Murray, originally from Hartlepool, has been in the army for twelve years. He's now in Belfast completing his fourth tour of duty there. Joss is crew commander on a Humber armoured personnel carrier, a one-ton armoured lorry which is one of the army's main modes of transport around Belfast. For windscreen the Pig (as it's known in army slang) has two slats; for rear window, an opening large enough to accommodate a 7.62 self-loading machine gun.

The main function of the Royal Corps of Transport, Joss's regiment, is to provide transport facilities for the rest of the army, whether it's in Belfast or Britain.

Joss's main assailants when he's inside the Pig seem to be children, who at the age of four have learned to throw abuse, bricks and rocks. From the inside of his armoured vehicle in Belfast, it must be a disheartening view of the world.

I find it very difficult to be happy in Belfast. I suppose I can laugh when I'm travelling in a Saracen (or a Pig) whilst the bottles of paint smash against the sides of the armour plating and the hundreds of bricks and stones hammer away at the steel shell. Yes, I can laugh in comparative safety. I can smile after someone spits at me and calls me a British bastard, but beneath the smile is a sadness. There are lots of good people in Ireland who are happy; because they are apart from those people that are filled with hatred.

Belfast apart, I find happiness in my letters from home. These are my consolation and I find happiness in the love that grows between myself and my wife Christine and in everything that we do and share. I find happiness in helping people genuinely in need.

When I finish my tour and I'm once again with my wife, when I get off the aircraft, a beautiful thing will happen, tears of happiness will be shed.

Alice Anne Parker

Alice Anne Parker's zodiac sign is Virgo with Gemini rising, and her moon in Pisces. Brought up in the United States, she graduated from Berkeley and went into the film industry, which brought her to England. Having studied the charts and books over a number of years, she set up as an astrological counsellor in 1973. You can go and visit her in Mayfair. She doesn't advertise, but just sees people who come as the result of personal recommendations – and she's very busy. A detailed birth chart is done for you and then she works as much from that as by clairvoyance. There's no set fee for a consultation – it's up to you to make your own donation. And she's a sympathetic and constructive person if you're in need of help or emotional support.

Puppies. Litters of puppies. I think puppies are one of the seven wonders of the world. The constant enthusiasm of dogs makes me happy, too.

Generally when I am happy I am thought-free, body-free, identity-free. It happens when I am working – doing readings, or when I vanish in some form of ecstasy about which I won't elaborate, or when I am doing creative work – the spine turns into a neon tube and time dissolves – that's one level of heaven.

Another level of heaven for me is pure sensation – not absence, but presence. Just one big tongue. Good ice cream can do that. I mean ice cream so good that you warm your tongue on the roof of your mouth between bites to open the taste buds up again. And contrasts. Lying on hot rocks after swimming in cold water. Popcorn, hot and buttery with champagne, icy and dry. Odd juxtapositions make me happy. Eating Japanese food in Rome. New Year's Eve at Brown's Hotel. I like collective nouns, too. A dazzle of zebras or a consolation of cookies.

It makes me happy not to know what's going to happen next month, or where I will be at this time next year. It may be only illusion, but I think to myself, what wonderful surprises can life have in store for me now?

Sister Georgina Payne

You feel dreadful, the food is awful, and they wake you up at an unfriendly hour. Yet no matter how much you complain about hospitals, their one saving grace is the nursing staff. Nurses work through the night, put up with us when we're making things difficult for them, and in our hour of need fill the role of ministering angels.

Up to the nineteenth century, most medical services were carried out by the religious orders. Florence Nightingale established nursing as a profession. In 1854, at the request of the secretary of war, she undertook the organizing and leading of a band of nurses to tend to the British army who were suffering serious injuries during the Crimean War. She succeeded in this task brilliantly, and returned to England a national heroine. Miss Nightingale then established the first school of nursing at St Thomas's Hospital in London, and the principles on which the school was founded ushered in the modern era of nursing. Among the novel concepts Florence Nightingale believed in was that nursing should be a full-time career.

Sister Georgina Payne has been a nurse for eight years. She works in the isolation ward at Farnborough Hospital, where such diseases as meningitis, whooping cough (which she caught), TB, hepatitis and other contagious diseases are treated. Gina is originally from Ilford. She has worked at Queen Mary's Hospital for Children, where she qualified as a nurse and trained in midwifery.

Being alone; walking the dog in the country
Surrounded by fields
Hot weather and the feel of sun on my skin and hair
Summer evenings, watching the stars in the sky
Autumn and the smell of smoke on Bonfire Night
Jacket potatoes oozing with butter
Receiving long letters from friends not seen often
Taking off in an aeroplane
Driving round London at night when there is no traffic
New-born babies and the expressions they make
A mother's expression when she sees her baby for the first time
Books and music
The car starting first time in winter
The look on children's faces as you tell them a story
Knowing a patient will recover when at times it's seemed impossible
Bubble baths and the feeling after a sauna
Visiting the dentist when no treatment is required
Looking at my old photographs
Watching a good suspense film
Church bells
Taking communion and knowing that God is real
Log fires and Christmas tree lights
Robins watching you as you dig over the garden
Making a bargain in the sales
Liqueur coffee after a delicious meal
Waking up to the knowledge that it's a day off from work.

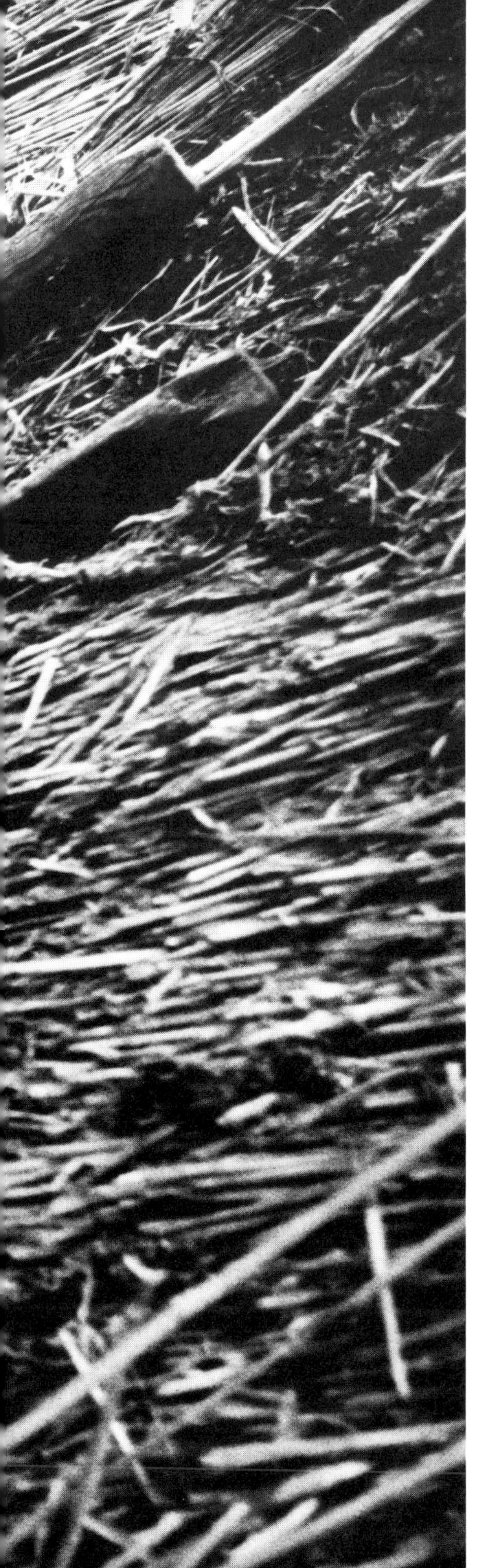

Jim Pearce

For 300 years the Pearce family have been thatchers in Wiltshire and it is unlikely that you would find a roof between Salisbury and Amesbury that wasn't thatched by Jim Pearce.

In 1929 Jim Pearce started to learn the trade from his father. His three brothers and two cousins were all thatching at that time.

It takes about ten years to learn how to thatch properly, Jim claims. He uses bundles of reeds from Somerset specifically grown for thatching and superior to straw.

On an average-sized cottage nearly four tons of reeds are used and a good thatch will last more than thirty years without repair. The insulation is much more effective than roof tiles. The house will stay cooler in the summer, and warmer in the winter.

When Jim started on his own he charged £40 a roof. Now it will cost more than £2,000. But there's no shortage of takers. Jim's diary is booked up for the next two years.

The thatcher usually works from right to left, begins at the eaves and works upwards. As a personal trademark, on top of every roof Jim thatches a straw pheasant.

I like to think I'm happy because I'm well satisfied with my lot. Thatching is our family trade and I've been doing it for fifty years, so I don't have to concentrate as hard as I used to. So very often I think of the happy days of my youth.

My three brothers and I lived near a canal. In the summer we fished and swam (a bit cloudy, the water became at times!). The canal froze over nearly every winter and then we scuffed along on rusty skates which were tied on with string.

When a rabbit was needed for a stew, our ferrets were put to work. A few weeks every spring were spent in the woods cutting hazel wood for thatching, and I well remember the beautiful wild flowers that grew under the oak trees, the mass of bluebells, the primroses, ragged robins, and many other smaller blooms.

People often stop at the front gate to admire my thatched birdtable – this keeps me happy.

Len Penrose

Len Penrose is the longest serving member of what is reputed to be the oldest (and without doubt the smallest) police force in the country.

There are six able-bodied men in the York Minster Police Force and their job is to protect the beautiful Minster in the centre of York. The force was set up in 1829 after a deranged sailor attempted (successfully) to set fire to the choir stalls. And it is believed that the YMPF inspired Sir Robert Peel, then Prime Minister, to set up a police force throughout the land.

Even after such a rich history, the powers of a York Minster policeman are not awesome. The ceremonial truncheon is bolted immovably to the wall in the east wing of the cathedral, and a citizen's arrest is the extent of their power.

Still, with three million visitors a year, crowd control is a heavy responsibility, and Len must be a brave man to stick the night shift alone in a dark, deserted cathedral.

When a lady asked Louis Armstrong what happiness was, he replied: 'Lady, if you have to ask you ain't got it.' But I disagree, happiness is something you earn, something you strive to achieve.

Appreciation of anything can only come when it is earned – in my personal view. Confucius, however, said there are many paths to the top of the mountain, but once there we all see the same moon. Even so, it's a stiff climb!

Mary Peters

International success in sport brings out the patriot in all of us – the British athlete standing taller than the also-rans, the Union Jack being raised while the National Anthem echoes defiantly through a foreign stadium.

So when a gold medal went to a British athlete at the Munich Olympics for the pentathlon, traditionally the most sought-after event to win, it made Mary Peters a household name.

Now Mary owns and runs a health club in Lisburn, just outside Belfast, helping people from all walks of life to stay fit. She has several mentally retarded members who train just as energetically as anyone else. She is also a manager of the British Olympic Team and coach to the pentathlon team.

The things which make me happy

The smell of spring flowers
A whole day without a telephone call
A warm lick from my dog Candy
Arriving home at Belfast Airport
The Antrim Coast road
Friendship
Children's laughter
A jog round the Mary Peters Track
My duvet
Brandy and lemonade
Soaking in the hydrotherapy pool
Meeting an old friend I haven't seen for ages
Spring flowers appearing in my own garden
A drive in my new car

Sheila Pickles

William Henry Penhaligon was the Court Barber during the reign of Queen Victoria. In the back of his shop he made perfumes, toilet waters and pomades. Today over a century later, Sheila Pickles, the current manager of Penhaligon's is preparing the fragrances from Mr Penhaligon's original notebooks.

The most expensive ingredient in Sheila's perfume is rose oil from the Valley of Roses in Bulgaria. It takes 4,000 roses to produce just one gram of oil and three metric tons to make one kilo. The finished product costs more than £4,000 and arrives at the shop in Covent Garden in a Securicor van.

Penhaligon make all their products on the premises. Aside from the scents, they make bath oils, candles, shampoo, soap and scented handkerchiefs. The smell is overpowering but delicious.

Fish and chips eaten on a park bench at midnight with a sweetheart gives me much more pleasure than dinner at the Ritz with a bore.

Reciprocal love makes me very happy; unrequited love on the other hand is almost the saddest thing I know. Very simple things give me an enormous amount of happiness, especially as this is a very romantic moment for me. Toasting marshmallows by a log fire with the man I love; lying on my chaise-longue looking down the garden listening to Al Bowlly singing *Songs for Sentimental Lovers* and dreaming; browsing round second-hand bookshops on a wet Saturday afternoon; having *Toad of Toad Hall* read to me in bed. I am an incurable potterer. No market stall or antique shop is safe, and what greater pleasure than finding some obscure knick-knack, doing it up and making it part of my home.

ENOCH POWELL

For Christmas this year, Mrs Powell is giving her husband a T-square, a glass cutter, and a pair of garden gloves. It's just what he wants, because Enoch Powell is an enthusiastic handyman who enjoys carpentry and home improvement. He is currently obsessed by picture framing, and will frame just about anything around the house he can lay his hands on.

Enoch Powell was born in Birmingham, the only child of two teachers. He won a scholarship to Cambridge, and at the age of twenty-five became a professor of Greek. During the war he spent three years in India where he learned to speak Urdu fluently. He left the army with the rank of brigadier.

Enoch Powell started a varied political career as Tory MP for Wolverhampton, became Minister of Health under Macmillan, and was an Opposition spokesman on transport and defence. He is now an Ulster Unionist MP.

Happiness is something that is not 'achieved' – it happens – whence, incidentally, the word itself. It can no more be achieved or 'pursued' (as in the American Declaration of Independence) than a chance meeting, or a stroke of genius, or a sunny day. Like everything that happens to man, it can be attributed alternatively to physical or to spiritual causes, and as usual both interpretations are true and not mutually exclusive. No doubt it is the consequence of a certain physical chemistry, either temporary or part of a person's natural endowment or both. No doubt also it is the result of 'grace', a thing given to us not of our merit or desiring, to which we cannot help but respond, like the morning stars when they 'sang together and all the sons of God shouted for joy'.

Marje Proops

Marje Proops has a lot of problems of her own right now. She went into hospital with a blocked artery and woke up with a small stroke. After a year and a half she still needs some help getting dressed. And she still has some paralysis of the right hand which means the amount of writing she can do is limited. She also suffers from arthritis of the hips and is waiting and hoping for a hip replacement operation. But Marje is fighting back. She now dictates all her copy either to her secretary or to a cassette recorder and she is back at her desk at the Daily Mirror *of which she's assistant editor, and once again taking control of the problems page which she has edited for more than twenty-five years.*

More than 30,000 letters arrive for 'Dear Marje', and it's hard, says Marje, to be on the receiving end of so much misery. She tries not to take the problems home, but inevitably she does get involved.

Happiness is being removed from the intensive care unit and being put in your own bed in a hospital.

Happiness is concerned nurses and skilled doctors who bring you back from the brink.

Happiness is being able to manage to cope with a boiled egg for breakfast. To learn to use a knife and fork again, to write your own name.

Happiness is going home to your family and knowing how much it means to them to have you back.

Happiness is going back to work when you thought you'd never see the place again.

In a word or two, it's a recognition of the simplest yet most important values of life – chief of which is life itself.

Magnus Pyke

Magnus Pyke OBE, FRIC, *F.Inst. Biol.*, FIFST, FRSE, *is everyone's favourite mad scientist. Ask him the time and he'll tell you how your watch works. Five years ago he was voted outstanding television newcomer at the age of sixty-seven. His science programme on TV has an audience of sixteen million and is probably the most popular science show ever. If you're curious as to what sort of tears crocodiles cry, why electricity makes your hair stand on end or the reason water always goes the same way down the plug hole – tune in to Magnus.*

During the war Magnus was an adviser on nutrition to the Ministry of Food, and he still retains a keen interest in the subject. He laments the unimaginative and wasteful practice in this country of limiting itself to a diet of only three common animals: fancy fricasse of dormouse, rhino rump, neck of giraffe – even perhaps old Pooch once he has laid down for good?

The secret of happiness is to be involved in some activity other than oneself, and to have a clear conscience. It matters little what the chosen activity is. It may be reconstructing antique clocks, writing books, running a corner shop or doing brain surgery. People immersed in such things are happy, people fretting about themselves are not. Yet the committed man, glancing up from his scientific research or his labours on behalf of the church fabric, and remembering that he has forgotten his wife's birthday, will feel a twinge of conscience. That is why good behaviour comes into the equation as well. But the happiest people are the busiest. Of all seven deadly sins, sloth is the most insidious. So go on collecting those butterflies.

Mary Rathmell

Halfway between Ilkley Moor and Leeds is the little town of Guisely, famous throughout Yorkshire not so much for its Saxon cross in the churchyard, nor its fine Elizabethan rectory, but for the best fish and chips in the country.

Over a million and a half customers a year patronize Harry Ramsden's Fish & Chip Shop, and by five-thirty of an afternoon when high tea is in full swing, there are often a hundred queuing outside.

Inside, the chandelier-lit restaurant with stained-glass windows is bursting with 300 hungry customers, but thanks to the efficient and nerveless coping of waitresses like Mary Rathmell, the crowd is kept in control.

Mary has been a waitress at Harry's for twenty-one years and loves the job, even at the most hectic hours.

What makes me happy? Oh so many things. My two wonderful sons and three grandchildren. I am a widow, and came to this home thirty-eight years ago as a bride. Living proof of my memories are small trees which were planted so long ago and bring me happiness. I was always told one is nearer to God's heart in a garden than anywhere else on earth.

I thought when my husband died I couldn't be happy again, but time does heal. Life is very different, but can still be full of happiness. My part-time job gives me lots of happiness. It's the type of work where one meets so many characters, where you get plenty of laughs, even without looking for them.

My husband and I worked for charity as 'Lions', it still makes me happy if I can help them as their work is so satisfying. I feel so well and energetic; health is better than any worldly goods.

Frances Robinson

With fourteen million people walking through the doors of its 252 stores every week, Marks and Spencer is without doubt the biggest retailer in the country. Take any ten women and six of them will be sporting St Michael's knickers. If they're wearing a bra, for one out of three that will be St Michael as well.

The High Street Empire had humble origins. Michael Marks, a Polish refugee, set up a penny bazaar in Leeds in 1884 (his catchphrase was 'Don't ask the price – it's a penny'). Business prospered as Marks opened stalls in market towns throughout the North, winning customers with the quality and good value he offered. In 1894 a partnership with Thomas Spencer, a cashier, was formed and the stalls grew into shops.

Marks and Sparks has 44,000 employees. We picked on Frances Robinson, assistant staff manageress at the Marble Arch store. With 860 workers there, it is the second largest store in the country.

Frances obtained a degree in psychology at Southampton University before taking the M&S one-year manager training course. She is responsible for recruiting and organizing staff, scheduling holidays, hiring temporary help in the busiest times. Since she left university she has got married and now commutes from Marlow in Buckinghamshire.

When I have achieved the goals I have set myself, whether it is completing a complex project at work or just a simple task like cleaning my house from top to bottom, the sense of satisfaction I gain makes me happy. In a different way lying on a palm-fringed coral beach in the sun or getting under a hot shower when I am cold and tired, or eating a delicious meal with a good bottle of wine all make me happy. These forms of contentment are all sensual in nature, and fairly transient, unlike the deeper sense of contentment I gain from a happy marriage and a satisfying job. I remember when my husband first gave me a single red rose, told me he loved me, and asked me to marry him. And then my most supremely happy wedding day, when I felt so excited I thought I would burst.

But there is nothing more rewarding than making someone else happy.

London Zoo

Harry Secombe

Harry Secombe's career, which has spanned everything from Goon humour to operatic aria, began in 1946 when he made his first professional stage appearance at London's Windmill Theatre. For £20 a week, six shows a day, six days a week, he did a routine imitating the various ways people shave. All the lather he had to use in his act did little for his complexion, and on rainy nights soap bubbles would rise from his hair.

During the war, Harry (who was promoted from company twit to division idiot) met Spike Milligan (Spike had lost an enormous 7.2 howitzer and had called on Harry for help), and after being demobbed he became friendly with Peter Sellers and Michael Bentine, and in 1951 they started the Goon Show.

Harry's Welsh background ensured a keen interest in singing, and he even had a number-one hit with 'This is My Song'. 'It was like Ben Hur winning the Grand Prix,' was his comment. Harry has appeared countless times at the Palladium, in television and films, even a serious West End play, and he remains one of the most versatile and popular performers in the country.

Happiness is a crisply folded, unread newspaper; the smell of bacon frying first thing in the morning. It is a little child taking my hand and leading me to meet his favourite toy; it is the sight of a white sail on a sparkling blue sea. It is the sound of children singing hymns and the feeling of satisfaction after a job well done. The knowledge that you are loved for what you are and not for what you pretend to be. But above all, happiness is, for me, having my wife and my children around me and my granddaughter on my knee.

David Shilling

David Shilling is mad about hats. From the age of six he was interested in them and at twelve he designed his first hat. The hats he makes for his mother to wear at Ascot are now an annual highlight of the races.

In David's shop in London's West End, hats come in all shapes, sizes and prices, starting at £60 and soaring to over a thousand for a little chinchilla number. In one corner there's a hat feathered in osprey and plumed in pheasant, a pink silk hat three feet across and two feet high; in another corner a hat mounted by two high-heeled shoes. Three of his hats reside at the Victoria and Albert as museum pieces.

Sadly for David, the era has passed when no gentleman would sally forth without his topper or at least a bowler, and a lady wouldn't be seen without her favourite bonnet.

But David, not yet thirty, thinks fashion will come to its senses and bring back that indispensable item – the hat.

From my first pot (silver of course) of China tea in the morning, through each bustling hat-making day, until I fall thankfully asleep, cosy in my gold and white bedroom under my mink quilt, I am truly happy.

On the odd bad day, however, when a feather won't curl, or I learn a headdress I've made won't be worn because they've called the wedding off, I turn to the list inside my head of 'happiness restorers'. I make a phone call to a close friend, organize tea at The Dorchester or Ritz, or scour a local junk shop. It is amazing how a few *marrons glacés* or a couple of bits of cheap music reverse a mood.

I'm not saying happiness can be bought, but it may be arranged.

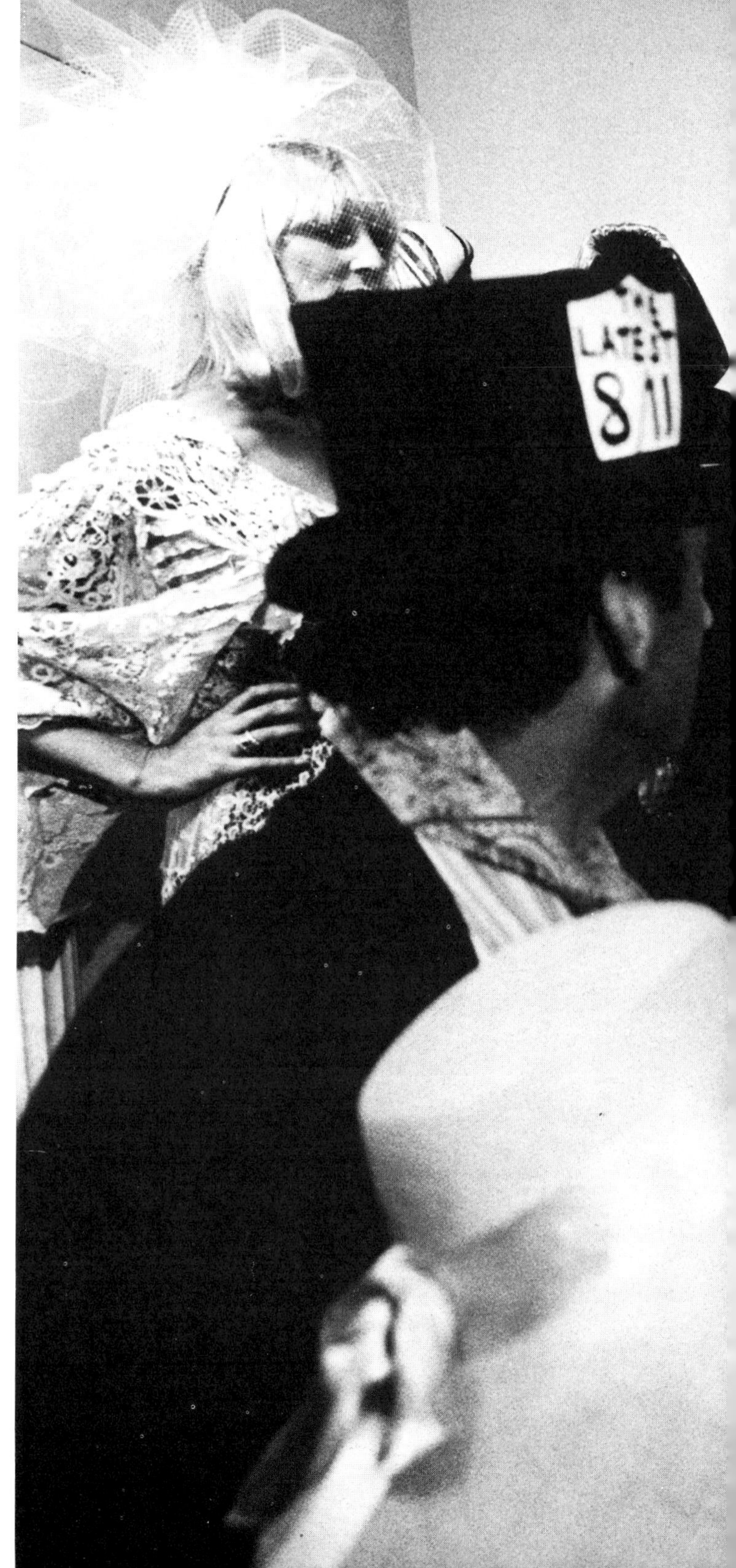

ALISTAIR SINCLAIR

There is a year's waiting list before you can get one of Alistair Sinclair's bagpipes. Together with his father and two craftsmen, Alistair turns out 200 sets a year in a suburb of Edinburgh. Alistair's bagpipes are made from African blackwood, one of the strongest woods in the world. The casing is made with sheep hide or cow skin, and the mountings can be fitted in plastic, ivory or silver. A set of pipes can cost anywhere from £200 to £2,000. Bagpipes are becoming increasingly popular. There have been orders from Canada, Australia and South Africa. It is said they blend well with the guitar. There are only five bagpipe makers in Scotland, and apprenticeship takes five years. There is great pride in the craftsmanship, and bagpipes should last for ever, Alistair says, so each of his instruments is unconditionally guaranteed.

I find happiness in my work as a bagpipe maker. Handling natural elements like wood and ivory is very rewarding. But I am happiest when I am at my place of worship. I love Jesus and therefore I am happy when I am with other people who love Him too. He is the only one who enables me to see joy and peace in this life. Without the knowledge that He has forgiven me for all the things I do wrong, I would be very unhappy indeed.

David Steel

David Steel's constituency is Roxburgh and Selkirk (known as the Borders). He tries to get home as often as possible, but it is all too seldom. His youngest son, Rory, once asked him in amazement as he saw him getting ready for bed: 'Daddy, are you staying here all night tonight?'

Home for the Steels is the tiny straggling village of Ettrick Bridge, near Selkirk. They have four children, one adopted four years ago.

David Steel spent four of the most formative years of his childhood in Kenya where his father (who later became Moderator of the Church of Scotland) had been posted as 'Minister of the Parish of East Africa'.

At Edinburgh University, David Steel had considered a legal career, and then spent a short period as a BBC interviewer, before entering politics. When he captured the Borders seat in a Scottish by-election, he was the youngest MP of the day, at twenty-six.

I like just to potter, to fish or walk in the beautiful Border hills with the dog. A warm loving home and unspoiled countryside are gifts to be treasured.

Erin Stratton

There's a peculiar species of bunnies in London's sporting Mayfair area, a breed that doesn't have long ears, or buck teeth and remained unscathed during the recent outbreak of myxomatosis.

The bunnies at the Playboy Club have two things in common – they are extremely attractive and they were handpicked by Erin Stratton, a sort of guardian or bunny mother to 300 girls.

Erin receives fifty letters a day from girls who want to become Playboy bunnies. She culls that list to thirty a week who then travel to London for an interview.

Bunnies come in all shapes (all shapely) and sizes; from 4′ 11″ to 6′ 2″, from 18 years old to 29, so the successful applicant needs a likeable personality as well as good looks.

Erin is an ex-bunny, so she knows the difficult aspects of bunny life. Wearing high heels on carpet for eight hours is a killer, and the costumes – which are skin-tight to begin with – become suffocating if a girl puts on even a couple of pounds. Erin instructs the girls in grooming, make-up and hair care.

Many things in my life make me happy; the closeness and love of my family, especially the newest addition, my nephew Oliver. My little dog Cromwell whose playful antics always keep me amused; not having to cook my own dinner when I get home from a hard day's work at the Club. All these things contribute to my happiness. But most of all happiness for me is waking up each morning full of enthusiasm.

Sheila Walker

The scouting movement began in 1908 when Lieutenant-General R.S.S. Baden-Powell, famous in Britain as the defender of Mafeking in the Boer War, wrote a book, Scouting for Boys, *for the purpose of training young men in the essentials of good citizenship. The movement immediately fired the imagination of boys throughout the world. Baden-Powell patterned the scouting uniform, and the slogan 'Be Prepared', after his own regiment, the South African Constabulary.*

It's probably fair to say that Baden-Powell never initially considered including girls in the scouting movement. But at the first rally of Boy Scouts at Crystal Palace, he was surprised to see a small group of 'Girl Scouts' – uninvited, unexpected and unwanted – marching past him for inspection. Impressed by their initiative, B-P asked his sister Agnes to take over the organization of the Girl Guides.

Sheila Walker, Chief Commissioner of the Girl Guides in Britain and the Commonwealth, is head of a movement that now boasts 900,000 members in this country alone, which is almost twice the number of Boy Scouts. Sheila was a Guide herself, although, she claims, a bad one. She is also a JP in Nottingham where she lives.

The scouting movement is still growing. World-wide, there are 8 million Girl Guides and 12 million Boy Scouts. Sheila is optimistic about today's youth, for she feels that scouting's essential ideas – the development of resourcefulness and initiative, encouragement of selflessness and helpfulness to others – remain as fundamental as when the movement began.

There is a beauty in intangibles, courage, kindness, loyalty and unselfishness, that lifts my heart. There is beauty in the shining faces of children, the eyes of dogs, the hands of artists and the feel of fur that stir a happiness inside. There are sounds that are so beautiful that the happiness from them almost hurts, and anyone who has been alone in a summer wood at dusk knows the utter contentment that comes from the beauty of nature.

The Duke of Westminster

There is a story, probably apocryphal, of when the Duke of Westminster was stopped by a policeman for speeding in Grosvenor Square. 'Think you own the bleeding place?' he was asked.

Not only does the Sixth Duke of Westminster, twenty-eight-year-old Gerald Cavendish Grosvenor, own the square, but a tidy 300 acre parcel of London which includes the south side of Oxford Street and 200 acres of Belgravia stretching from Knightsbridge to Pimlico (which the family had to sell off to pay death duties). With enormous landholdings in Cheshire, N. Ireland, Wales, Hawaii, Canada, Australia and America, Gerald Grosvenor is possibly the wealthiest man in the world, with a fortune that at the meagrest guess starts at five hundred million pounds.

As head of the Grosvenor Trust, he works long hours to safeguard his heritage. Married with a one-year-old daughter, he commutes from his ancestral home in Chester to the London office by helicopter. Gerald is not a man to rest on his family's laurels, and it is no surprise to learn of the family motto: Virtue not Ancestry.

Being alone with my wife in the privacy of my own home is something I value above all; to love and respect one's parents, to always know that they are not far away when you really need them. I consider myself fortunate to have had a stable family, who have taught me that *real* love and *real* happiness can never be bought.

Barbara Wieshoff

Barbara Wieshoff's whole life is the circus. Her mother was an acrobat. Her father is a wild-animal trainer and her husband a former trapeze artist. Her brother was tragically mauled to death by a lion.

Having tried practically every circus act, trained lions, giraffes, elephants, and kangaroos, it wasn't until she started working with chimpanzees that Barbara felt she'd found her métier.

Freddie, the big chimp, Louise and Topaz are treated like treasured children. Porridge for breakfast, fruit or salad for lunch, chicken soup with noodles and baked potato for dinner was on the menu the day we met the family. And if the chimps have been well behaved they might get their favourite food – strawberry lollipops.

For nine months of the year Barbara tours all over the country in her motorized caravan with the Gerry Cottle Circus. With two shows a day, sometimes three on Saturdays and Sundays and public holidays, it's a lot of hard work. But for circus people that is the only way of life they know, and they wouldn't trade it for any other.

I am happiest when I am with my animals, because I know my animals want me to be with them to help and care for them.

In the morning, when I bring them breakfast they greet me with hugs and kisses like a long-lost member of their family. Nobody in your own human family would greet you with more affection!

The work my chimps do in the circus is not work in the true sense of the word, it is more an outlet for their intelligence and energy. They like doing things on their own and I give them a pretty free run. Anybody watching them in the ring will agree with me. They enjoy themselves!

In the evening, they will say goodnight to me in their own language. Just being with my animals is happiness for me!

James Alfred Wight

James Alfred Wight hadn't written a word in his life until, at the age of fifty, he decided to chronicle his adventures as a vet in the Yorkshire Dales. Challenged by his wife Helen who said men of his age didn't write books, it took him more than a year to complete his first book, typing a few hours a night after work. Watching football on TV one evening, he saw a goalkeeper for Birmingham City dive to make a spectacular save. The goalkeeper's name was Herriot, and James Wight decided to make it his pseudonym.

James was born in Glasgow, and despite an urban upbringing, dreamed as a child of becoming a vet. After qualifying at the Glasgow Veterinary College at twenty-four, he moved to a little Yorkshire market town in the Dales which he has made his home for the past forty years. His son works in the veterinary practice with him, and his daughter is a doctor in the town.

It seems surprising that a man whose books are bestsellers all over the world, who has had two films and a television series based on his life, should remain unimpressed and untainted by all this attention. And yet, at sixty-four, James Herriot is still a working vet.

We need look no further than James Herriot's books which sell in their millions to confirm that this is a country of animal lovers, although it is ironic that vets belong to one of the lowest-paid professions. James claims he would have been 'on his uppers' if the first book hadn't sold.

The happiest man in my orbit is a casual farm labourer called Fred Belling who hasn't a penny in the world, nor has he a care. He is a bachelor, works when he feels like it and, due to his devotion to beer and constant small investments with the local bookies, has always got through his wages by Wednesday of every week. He has no home and eats and sleeps where he can, but he also has no mortgage, bank overdraft or insurance policies to disturb his dreams. I often see him strolling along the country lanes in the mornings, whistling on his way to work. This might be as late as ten o'clock, because if Fred has a hangover he abandons any idea of six a.m. milking.

In my early days as a young vet with a family I had either to work round the clock or starve, and it was during those hard days when I spent every waking hour dashing around the Yorkshire countryside, usually with my children in the car, that happiness seemed to steal up behind me and tap me on the shoulder.

I am often touched when people write to say that my books have made them laugh and perhaps pulled them through a bad period and I find a wry humour in the fact that I read these letters with my morning tea when I am sometimes feeling very low myself. I am reminded repeatedly that we all have our problems.

Money, success, the approbation of the world – these things have nothing to do with happiness, in fact they more often destroy the peace of mind which is man's greatest blessing.

Even Fred Belling experiences times of black depression when a cast-iron treble comes unstuck or the draught bitter at his local turns sour in hot weather, and surely it is the greatest comfort to all of troubled humanity to realize one profound truth: that nobody is happy all the time.

Died, 2nd December 1920.
erected by his Son and Daughter-in-law.
IN THE TRANSVAAL.
THE REGIMENTAL DISTRICT, HOUNSLOW
FROM 1902 TO 1909
AND THE HOME COUNTIES AND WESSEX TERRITORIAL
DIVISIONS FROM 1908 TO 1914.
SERVED IN THE GREAT WAR AS INSPECTOR OF THE
TERRITORIAL ARMY IN INDIA FROM 1914 TO 1915.
GENERAL OFFICER COMMANDING,
WESTERN RESERVE CENTRE, FROM 1915 TO 1917.
BORN 18TH SEPTEMBER 1854: DIED 31ST OCTOBER 1939
AGED 85 YEARS.
THIS TABLET WAS ERECTED BY HIS WIFE.
RH

Frederick Trevor Woods

There are a group of men who still have cause to be grateful to Nell Gwynne. For it was she who persuaded King Charles II to build a hospital for retired soldiers. And Charles, who found it difficult to deny Miss Gwynne her slightest wish, was glad to oblige.

The 400 veterans who reside at the Royal Hospital, Chelsea, are called Chelsea Pensioners. It is less a hospital, in the conventional sense, than a residence for retired soldiers. There are long-established criteria for entry to the Royal Hospital. Applicants must be from the non-commissioned ranks; sixty-five years of age or older; in possession of an army pension for long service or disability, and free of family commitments. There is always a waiting list, and openings occur through death.

Many of the men are First World War veterans, and there are even those who fought the Boer War, which makes the Royal Hospital a living historical archive.

At seventy-seven, Sergeant Frederick Trevor Woods is a relative youngster. Fred left school at fourteen to help supplement the family income by working as an under-gardener. Later he helped his father in the family boot and shoe repairing company. In 1922, Fred joined 'the best outfit in the army', the West Yorkshire Regiment. Within three years Fred took over control of the officers' mess, and before the Second World War was promoted to the rank of Company Quartermaster-Sergeant. Fred travelled around the entire world, and in 1942 served under Field-Marshal 'Bill' Slim in Rangoon. Having caught malaria out in Burma, Fred was sent to a holding and posting company in England until the end of the war. He then joined the Shropshire Army Cadet force, training young men for the army until he became sixty-five, and was awarded, on retirement, an MBE.

Knowing that since I was the age of twelve I have worked hard, played hard and used the years usefully, helped other people whenever I could and looked to the future instead of the past, this makes me happy. I've not overspent my money, saved what I could, and arrive at the age of seventy-seven with only happy memories, a little capital which allows me to do some of the things I have always yearned to do, and if necessary to help others.

I have a nice home, a very pleasant little job, am surrounded by nice people, lovely grounds to wander in, good food, and my health.

What more could I wish for and who could say with truth that I could be otherwise happy?

Mike Worden

In the tiny Cornish village of Stratton, Mike Worden is the local carpenter, plumber, painter and plasterer. But the biggest part of his business and the most strenuous has little to do with home repairs, because Mike is also the village undertaker.

Naturally death makes him sad, especially as he knew most of the people he has had to bury – his own father who was also the village undertaker and carpenter lies in a corner of the graveyard – but he says that dealing with death makes him enjoy life all the more and so he will never put off anything he could do today for another moment.

The biggest funeral Mike undertook was when the Vicar of Stratton who was also the Canon of Truro died. More than fifty vicars attended the ceremony.

An interesting fact Mike told us is that lay people are buried facing west, but churchmen lie towards the east – thus on the day of reckoning the priest will be able to instruct his congregation.

Mike has three daughters so it appears the family business will end with him – but as there is little space left in the graveyard at St Andrew's of Stratton, Mike is convinced that bodies will have to be cremated in a short time.

My work as a builder and undertaker necessitates me being constantly on call by those in need – but herein lies another source of happiness to me. This is a paradox – I see grief and sorrow at first hand, but in acting for people at a time of bereavement I achieve happiness through the satisfaction of helping to the best of my ability those in need.

I also find happiness in simple pleasures – a pint at the local in convivial company, listening to music, enjoying a good meal, but above all enjoying the peace and solitude to be found in the countryside observing the beauty and wonder of nature, whether it be a walk in the hills of Shropshire or Derbyshire or a stroll in winter across the deserted beaches on the North Cornish coast.

Bill Wright

Bill Wright seems like quite a nice man. You wouldn't guess he's the originator of the most demanding quiz that has ever appeared on television. But he is the one on whom blame can be squarely placed. He is extremely proud of what he considers to be the most exciting, exacting and erudite quiz that not only gives entertainment to millions but also gives a mass of information.

Bill Wright is the producer of Mastermind, *a television programme watched by thirteen million people for the past nine years, in which ordinary people like you and me – well, perhaps a little brainier – are placed in a black chair and grilled on some obscure specialist subject such as nineteenth-century beauty spots on the Isle of Man or seven-letter words in the Old Testament.*

Bill worked his way up the ladder of the BBC, starting as a pageboy at Broadcasting House in 1936. He became a cameraman, stage manager, and sports and science producer before he dreamed up Mastermind.

From 3,000 applications a year, Bill whittles down the list to 300 or 400 people whom he auditions personally. Their logic, concentration, ability to have inspired guesses and even courage are assessed. Finally, forty-eight contestants are chosen and the fun begins.

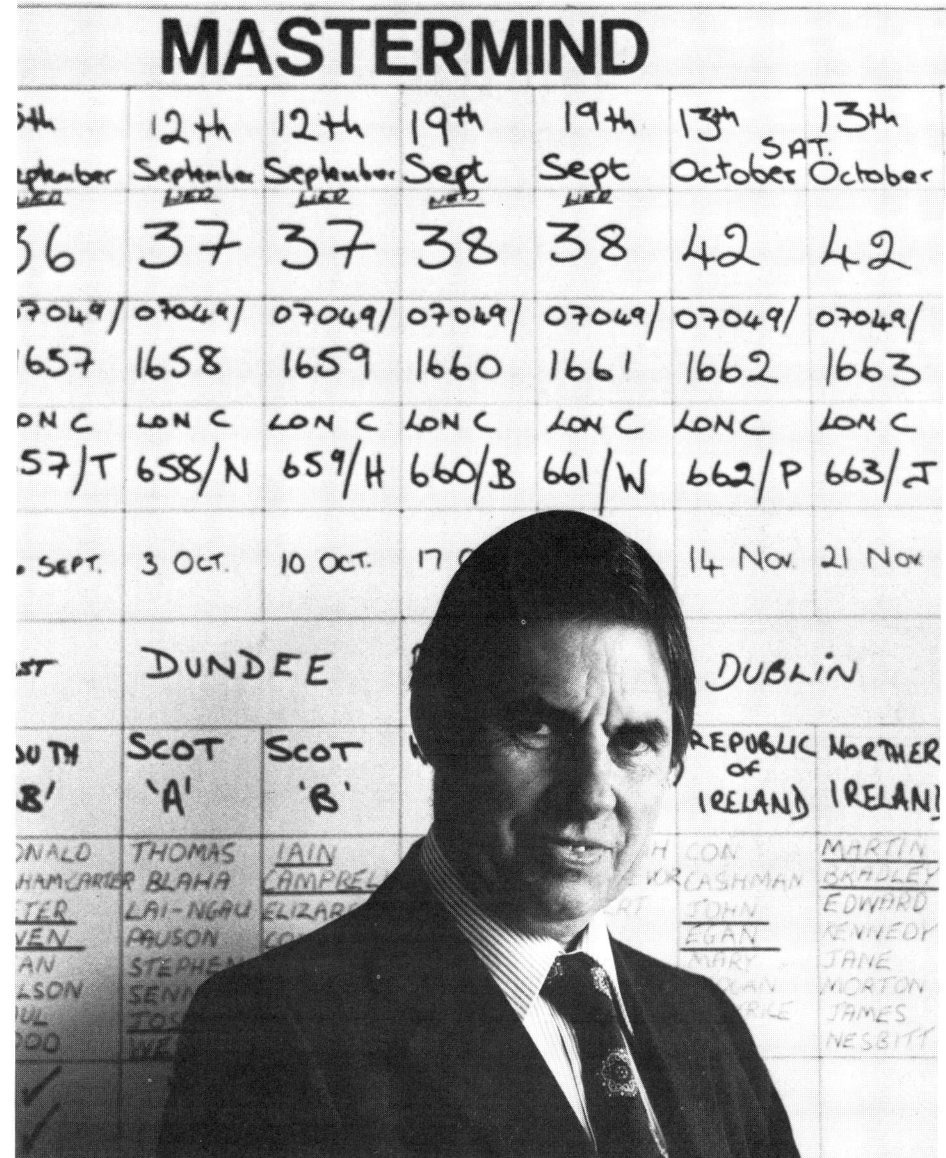

Music is a large key to my happiness, but it has to be classical and live. I prefer the Russian composers, with Shostakovich heading the list with his wonderful Symphony No. 5, which for me is the symphony of life itself. When I listen to this work played by an orchestra at the Royal Festival Hall I am lifted into another dimension, and the happiness that results I can only describe as a kind of unity with all aspects of the universe.

People, too, give me great happiness and I am most fortunate that *Mastermind* allows me to bring people together from all walks of life, sharing, as they do, with each other at the time of the contest the common factors of concentration and comradeship. Win or lose, most of them derive a happiness from having shared in this unique experience.

Father Xmas

For more years than he cares to remember, Father Xmas has been making 25 December a favourite fixture in everyone's diary. In the BC millenia it was hard to get much of a party atmosphere going at the end of the year – office parties revolved around the equinox or harvesting. But once Christianity started to spread, Christmas took on a whole new meaning.

Preparation for the Christmas season has always been a full-time occupation for St Nick (he was canonized several centuries ago for services to industry) but he seems to have more work to do every year. Kids expect more; electronic gifts and sophisticated games are de rigeur *even for the youngest children, and with a Christmas spirit that is increasingly more commercial than spiritual, the Yuletide season is at its height of popularity.*

Home for Santa is still the North Pole, although as he gets older he has been looking at real estate in warmer climes. However, it's unlikely he'll move – the public would have trouble adjusting to such a radical change of image, and the reindeer would not enjoy the heat.

What makes me happy? It's a funny question to ask – me of all people. My life has been spent making others happy, I can't think of a more rewarding occupation than that.

Imagine the scene: a clear, frosty night, the stars twinkling, Prancer, Dancer and the whole team hovering noisily above the chimney tops, their breath smoking in the cold air, their bells and harnesses making clanging Christmas music. Down the chimney I swoop, and fill the stockings full of toys. I can't stay around to be thanked – but the knowledge that on Christmas Day everyone is merry and cheerful, that families unite and a feeling of friendship and goodwill envelops the human race – that gives me a happiness that has kept me alive all these years and will continue to do so as long as there is love in the world.